ACTING RIGHT

Building a Cooperative, Collaborative, Creative Classroom Community Through Drama

SEAN LAYNE

FORESIGHT BOOK PUBLISHING
ForesightPublishingNow.com

A GOOD TRIP IS NEVER TAKEN ALONE.

*This book is dedicated to four trailblazing women
who made this journey possible:*

Lenore Blank Kelner, who invited me to begin the walk.

*Amy Duma, who provided the maps, and gear, and
opportunities for me to remain on the path.*

*Lynne Silverstein, who helped me prune the shrubs, name the
plants, and reflect on my surroundings along the way.*

*And Melanie Rick, who helped me choose a direction when
I encountered forks in the path, and encouraged me when it
would have been easier to sit down or turn around.*

ACKNOWLEDGEMENTS

My humble acknowledgements to the thousands of students who have helped me define and shape this work. There were many days I got it wrong. Thank you for your patience. There were many days I got it right. Thank you for your smiles, hugs, and letters of appreciation.

I would like to acknowledge the hundreds of teachers I have trained and observed implementing the work. I never cease to be inspired by your commitment to the students and the field of education. You have helped me refine and clarify this work.

I would also like to acknowledge the incredibly gifted, talented, and reflective team of *Focus 5, Inc.* consultants that have tirelessly and joyfully shared this work in schools across the country. Beth, Kassie, Jamin, Carrie, Jason, Jennifer, Rebecca, Paige, Marlo and Solomon, your passion for the arts and for education fuel this work and change lives.

And finally, I want to acknowledge my family at *Focus 5, Inc.* that make this work possible. Melanie, Michelle, Eileen, and Raelyn- your dedication, organization, sense of humor, and love create the space necessary for me to create, soar, fail, and explore in such a safe and supportive environment. Thank you for being part of this wild ride.

TABLE OF CONTENTS

PREFACE

"I am no longer afraid of becoming lost, because the journey back always reveals something new, and that is ultimately good for the artist."

— Billy Joel

Teaching students productive classroom behavior through drama. *That is the focus of Acting Right.*

What connection does acting have with learning? What does an actor know about teaching and behavior? Three decades of working with thousands of students and teachers across the nation have given me some answers to those questions. Although students are naturally social beings, on the whole they do not know how to interact within the classroom community in ways that support collaboration and learning. Students needed to be explicitly taught how to channel their attention and concentration for effective learning.

I have had the opportunity to observe the social dynamics of classroom communities in almost every type of learning environment and to test and hone strategies that help students develop the necessary skills for becoming effective learners within a community. This book shares a part of what I have learned, developed, and refined in my work in countless classrooms as a teaching artist.

> **Because of my beliefs about learning, I needed students to leave their seats and form small groups. The seated, isolated, and silent environment needed to be transformed into a learning environment that was social, active, cooperative, and collaborative.**

Here's how my journey began. I started my career in the arts as a professional actor for InterAct Story Theatre, a touring educational theatre company founded and directed by Lenore Blank Kelner. Not only did we perform plays for students, we went into classrooms to guide students in creating and performing theatrical pieces focused on an area of the curriculum they were studying. The work was creative, educational, and immensely rewarding and would set me on a career path in arts integration.

My work in these classrooms highlighted some important issues. As I entered classrooms, the approach to teaching seemed fairly consistent: the teacher was standing at the front of the room, doing most of the talking, and students were seated at desks. Attention, participation, and engagement on the student's part was scattered and varied. The learning was very independent. As a teaching artist, bringing the arts into the classroom, I knew my approach to teaching was different. I needed students to work collaboratively and cooperatively, to be able to focus their attention, to self-regulate their behavior, and to be active, creative learners.

Because of my beliefs about learning, I needed students to leave their seats and form small groups. The seated, isolated, and silent environment needed to be transformed into a learning environment that was cooperative, collaborative, and creative.

This shift, unfortunately, was usually marked by varying degrees of chaos because many classes did not know how to handle the freedom of movement or the opportunity to be social in a constructive way. My early strategies caused an explosion of physical energy, unfocused attention, and uncontrolled emotions. Students did not know how to interact, concentrate, or cooperate in a learning environment. They were not in a state of mind that promoted, or even allowed, learning. What was most surprising to me, however, was that most students did not have the skills to reflect on their own thinking and behavior. In these early attempts, drama, which is a powerful and effective tool for learning, often was ineffective, disruptive, and unmanageable.

I could have blamed the students. Instead, I recognized that if I wanted or expected certain behaviors from students, it was my responsibility to teach them. This led me to the question, "What do I need to teach to students that will allow them to participate effectively in active, social learning?" I reflected on my acting training and the answer surfaced. Actors begin their training participating in team-building exercises that build ensemble and camaraderie with their fellow actors. I realized that I had skipped that team-building step when I went into classrooms. I had assumed those prerequisite skills had already been established. This realization ultimately changed the course of my career. If I wanted a social, cooperative, and creative classroom community, I would need to develop strategies to teach students those skills.

With this realization, I founded an arts integration consulting company, Focus 5, Inc., and initiated my search for the building blocks for teaching and honing the behavioral and social skills students needed to learn productively. The challenge was to find ways to assess whether the students had the skills to concentrate, cooperate, self-regulate, and collaborate. They couldn't successfully participate in learning through drama without them.

The focus of my work emerged—to develop indicators of readiness and arts-integrated drama strategies for strengthening behavior and providing ways for students to show they were, as I termed it, Acting Right. I took the foundational elements of acting—those fundamental skills of concentration, cooperation, and collaboration—and created a structured process that became the basis for effective classroom management in grades K-12. The four cornerstone strategies of this step-by-step approach are:

- *The Actor's Toolbox*
- *The Concentration Circle*
- *The Cooperation Challenge*
- *One-Minute Challenge Tableau*

To develop the Acting Right approach, I reviewed standard acting warm-ups and games and revised them for the purposes of teaching and assessing behavior. I modified and created game-like, theatre-based exercises that would help students to develop positive behaviors. My initial steps in using the strategies were small and unsteady, but teachers responded positively to them right from the start. Their encouragement fueled my continued efforts.

To further develop and hone the Acting Right approach, I spent a great deal of time over the years observing students—hundreds and hundreds of students—looking for patterns in their responses to the strategies. My training as an actor taught me

My approach to teaching developed over time and is marked by these beliefs:

Learning is COLLABORATIVE

Students often work in groups, learning from and with their peers. I encourage learning-focused conversation between and among students and challenge groups to develop and refine their ability to cooperate.

Learning is EXPERIENTIAL

Students engage in learning by doing. They work both hands-on and minds-on. They may be out of their seats and moving to learn. The learning environment must be flexible, with furniture rearranged or removed for our purposes.

Learning is ACTIVELY BUILT

Students create their own understanding. Learning is not passive. I ask many questions to help students form their own understandings, rather than giving them the answers.

Learning is PROBLEM-SOLVING

The arts engage students in the creative process, which naturally involves them in imagining, asking questions, exploring, creating, reflecting, revising, and generating and sharing novel solutions. Although I guide students work, I do not tell students exactly how to do something. I encourage them to create appropriate solutions.

Learning is EVOLVING

Learning takes place over time. The creative process does not begin and end in a 45-minute class session. It requires time to ponder, revisit, revise, and experiment. I recognize the evolving nature of the creative process and remain flexible to the students' needs.

Learning is REFLECTIVE

Learning requires that students pause and think in ways that transform their understandings. Students must look back at their experiences and reflect on their learning in various ways—by talking with each other, sharing their ideas with me, and in writing.

to observe social interactions—motivations for and the cause and effect of actions. That training proved to be quite useful in the classroom. I compared student behaviors across classrooms, attempting to decipher why certain classroom communities were different and why others were similar. When my efforts were successful, I would reflect on exactly why the strategies were working. My goal was to refine the strategies so they would work across grade levels and in a wide range of classroom environments.

Needless to say, it took a long time to test and perfect the strategies in scores of different types of classrooms with highly diverse student populations. During the process, I observed that when students work together as a group—an ensemble as it is called in the arts—they learn to pick up on one another's positive energy. I saw how positive peer pressure could be used to create a cohesive and supportive group, and how it could counteract unproductive behaviors when they surfaced. Additionally, the Acting Right strategies develop teachers' abilities to recognize and respond to the behavior choices student make in their interactions with you, their peers, and the activities.

> **The strategies enable students to build the skills necessary for establishing a sense of self-control, accountability, and camaraderie in their classrooms.**

This engaging step-by-step approach empowers a wide range of students to take ownership of and be responsible for their behavior. The strategies enable students to build the skills necessary for establishing a sense of self-control, accountability, and camaraderie in their classrooms. The Acting Right approach also empowers teachers by giving them three gifts—the language, energy, and strategies—that enable them to be productive instructional leaders, while at the same time establishing and maintaining a positive classroom community.

Throughout the developmental work, I read a range of literature focused on behavior. I noticed that much of my process and work aligned with best practices in teaching, sociology, and classroom management. I was also fortunate enough to collaborate closely for many years with a very talented, national board-certified teacher and reading specialist, Melanie Rick, who also holds a degree in special education. At the time, she was working in an extremely diverse school with a wide range of cultures, academic abilities, and special needs. So, while I was working in many classrooms nationwide for brief periods of time, I was able to have ongoing, long-term contact with her class for many years. These on-going interactions with one classroom over the course of a school year, coupled with the opportunity to reflect with a highly-accomplished educator, proved to be invaluable in refining the Acting Right strategies.

Another relationship that was invaluable to the development of the work was with Amy Duma, Director of Teacher and School Programs at the John F. Kennedy Center for the Performing Arts in Washington, D.C. The Acting Right strategies were, and continue to be used extensively in the Kennedy Center's Changing Education Through the Arts program (CETA). This program afforded me the opportunity to see the effects of my work school-wide and not just in one school, but in many. The teachers and administrators in these schools, along with the guidance and support from the Kennedy Center, helped to shape how this work transferred to whole school implementation and how the work ultimately could be designed for teachers' professional learning.

Educators' response to Acting Right has been overwhelming. Eventually, the demand for this work exceeded what I could deliver alone. Now I have a team of highly-skilled consultants who share the Acting Right strategies in schools throughout the nation. The work they are doing to impact student growth and teacher professional learning contributes to the ongoing development and refinement of the Acting Right strategies.

Teaching behavior through an arts-integrated approach has redefined my career and my perspective of what students are capable of achieving. Early in my teaching, I was standing on a relatively small stage, focused on bringing the excitement and power of drama to students. Not only is the impact of the arts for learning much richer than I originally imagined, my experiences have revealed a much richer mission that has pushed me onto a much bigger stage—bigger than I ever imagined. My goal with the Acting Right strategies outlined in this book is to help educators transform their classroom communities into a state of collective calm energy, focused minds, and balanced emotions—a place where students will not only achieve greater academic success through arts-integrated learning, but will also achieve personal growth that holds tremendous promise for their lives beyond the classroom.

ACTING RIGHT:
CORE BELIEFS

"If the end in view is the development of a spirit of social co-operation and community life, discipline must grow out of and be relative to such an aim...and out of doing these in a social and cooperative way, there is born a discipline of its own kind and type."

— John Dewey

BEHAVIOR IS A LITERACY

Classroom management is a hot topic in education and teachers have found many ways to manage behaviors—from marking behavior charts, to flipping cards over from the green to red, to passing out reward "bucks." The list goes on. The problem is teachers are trying to manage something that has never been taught.

Many teachers, both new and experienced, view student behavior as something they have to "manage" or "control." We might compare teachers' efforts to manage behavior with the arcade game Whack-a-Mole, in which players use a mallet to hit fake moles as they appear randomly out of their holes. When one mole is whacked and retreats into its hole, another one pops up. Many teachers simply "whack" down the problem behavior. Inevitably, it just pops up again.

In math classes, we do not hesitate to correct students when their solution to a problem is incorrect. If students calculate 2+2=5, without hesitation we let them know that answer is incorrect and we guide them to calculate the answer correctly. In a writing assignment, if students incorrectly use "your" instead of "you're," we circle the word, calling it to the students' attention. We correct these mistakes in the moment because we know that math and reading, along with other curriculum areas, are literacies that are learned through modeling and repetition. Without these corrections, students who add incorrectly or whose grammar is incorrect will, most likely, continue to make these mistakes. Additionally, teachers are patient and persistent in teaching mathematics and grammar. Teachers accept that numeracy and reading are literacies that need to be taught, retaught, and learned over time.

Why then, do we respond differently to problem behavior? Why do many teachers become frustrated when inappropriate behavior surfaces in the classroom and in some cases, even hesitate to correct it?

To me, behavior is as a literacy that can be taught with patience and strengthened over time through practice and repetition.

The goal of the Acting Right strategies is not to manage behavior, but to teach behavior. When we accept this premise, we have greater patience and persistence in shaping behaviors. We also see greater and faster change in students' behaviors. Students feel empowered and proud as they master self-regulation and develop and expand their capacity to learn in social and active ways.

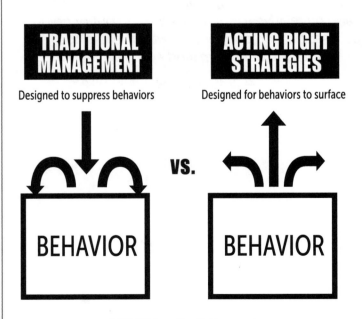

TRADITIONAL MANAGEMENT

Designed to suppress behaviors

ACTING RIGHT STRATEGIES

Designed for behaviors to surface

VS.

BEHAVIOR | BEHAVIOR

If we are teaching behavior, then we must be able to assess students' initial skill set before we plan the appropriate next steps. To do that, the Acting Right strategies bring a range of behaviors to the surface, allowing you to identify strengths and weaknesses and allowing students to see behaviors in action so they can learn to differentiate between the productive and non-productive ones and learn to self-regulate their behavior. In contrast, some traditional classroom management strategies aim to suppress behaviors.

There are two important aspects to teaching behavior effectively. The first is through questioning and reflection. There was a time in education when teaching was synonymous with lecturing, also known as "sit and get." This passive approach was based on the idea that students were empty vessels and teachers could simply pour information into their heads. But now we know that is not how learning works. We know that students learn better when we guide them to construct their own understandings. Through open-ended questions and reflection, students become more capable of thinking about their thinking and the behaviors that follow from those thoughts (a metacognitive skill). Students learn to be aware of when they use a reactive behavior, what triggered the behavior, and ultimately how to stop unproductive behaviors.

I think of learning this way—students should do the "heavy lifting." In other words, students should be given the responsibility of thinking about their behavior. Often, when we tell students what to do and how to do it, we rob them of opportunities to think for themselves and to consider and adjust their behaviors. Simply adhering to a teacher's directive to "stop talking," does not engage students in the "heavy lifting." Instead, we must challenge students to think about why they were behaving in a particular way and why that behavior is counterproductive.

> **We know that students learn better when we guide them to construct their own understandings.**

A huge shift happens when students are asked to identify the unproductive behavior they are exhibiting. The shift deepens when students are asked how their behavior is disrupting the others' learning. When students construct their own understandings about behavior, when they "connect the dots" themselves, they will be able to consider their behavior without relying on us to do it for them. The Acting Right strategies align with this empowerment approach, helping students to become more self-reliant and confident learners.

A second important aspect of teaching behavior is frequency of use. Teachers often ask how frequently they should use the strategies outlined in this book. I often offer the analogy of going to the gym. If you go to the gym once a week for ten minutes, what will happen? Not very much, at least not quickly. But if you go to the gym every day for 30 minutes, you'll definitely see changes in your strength. Going two hours a day will result in even greater changes at an even faster rate. The Acting Right strategies focus on cooperation, concentration, and collaboration, all of which are like muscles that can be developed and strengthened depending on how much and how long you use them. So, the question isn't how often should you use the strategies, but rather how fast do you want students to develop these skills? The answer to the latter will determine your frequency of use.

CALM BODY + FOCUSED MIND + BALANCED EMOTIONS = READINESS TO LEARN

Research in brain-based learning, social-emotional learning, and mindfulness points to the need for students to be in a state of mind, or readiness, for deep, lasting learning to occur[1]. Drawing from those areas of research, along with my experience working with hundreds of classrooms, I have distilled the findings into three states of readiness for Acting Right:

Calm — *refers to the body*

Focus — *refers to the mind*

Balance — *refers to the emotions*

When the body is calm, the brain is focused and our emotions are balanced, we are ready for learning. If one of these states of readiness is missing, the capacity to learn is diminished. Because arts-integrated learning is cooperative, collaborative, and creative, it is imperative that students come to the work in a calm, focused, and balanced state. When working with a group of students, our first question should be: "Is the group in front of me calm, focused, and balanced?" If the answer is no, then we need to do something to get them into that state of readiness, or their learning will be compromised. The Acting Right strategies calm the students' bodies, focus their minds, and balance their emotions. Increasingly, educators are seeing the need for mindful, brain-based approaches to learning, like the Acting Right strategies. These approaches are grounded in what we know about the brain. Research findings suggest that achieving a calm, focused, and balanced state changes how the brain responds to stress, possibly building the brain's neural connections, reducing its reactivity, and thus setting the stage for reflection and self-regulation[2].

> **The Acting Right strategies calm the students' bodies, focus their minds, and balance their emotions.**

Further, learning requires students to focus their minds and reject impulses toward distraction. According to the Caine Learning Institute[3], learning requires focused attention, among other things. Students' ability to focus their attention requires that they ignore some of the stimuli that are peripheral to their needs at a given moment. Consider the multiple types of stimuli that can divert attention in a classroom. Depending on the classroom culture, the challenges to focused attention can be minor or considerable. Acting Right teaches students to focus their attention.

In short, with the stresses of everyday life, many students arrive at school unready to learn. This creates the need to take time to deliberately help students calm their minds and bodies using mindful, social-emotional strategies like Acting Right. We must teach rather than manage behavior.

LEARNING REQUIRES A REFLECTIVE RATHER THAN REACTIVE RESPONSE

Consider that our behavior is controlled by an emotional "switching station" in the brain. We respond in one of two ways—with a reactive response or a reflective response. The reactive response subverts learning. In contrast, the reflective response supports learning.

Reactive Response. From the field of psychology, we know that there are three indicators of a reactive response—fight, flight, and freeze. These indicators identify how we are likely to react when a situation overwhelms our coping capacity.

- FIGHT Response – *If students assess a situation as something they have the power to defeat, they go into fight mode. Acting out verbally or physically are indicators that students are in fight mode.*

- FLIGHT Response – *If students assess a situation as too powerful to overcome, their impulse is to run. Disengaging from a lesson or disengaging from a group (whether mentally or physically), are indicators that students are in flight mode.*

- FREEZE Response – *If students assess a situation as something they can neither defeat nor run from, they go into freeze mode. Shutting down and not responding at all are indicators that students are in freeze mode.*

It is important to note that if students switch to a reactive response during class, it is typically a subconscious reaction to some trigger rather than a deliberate choice. Generally, this reaction is hard for students to correct because they are usually unaware of the trigger. Here, the Acting Right strategies align with cognitive behavior therapy, which is a process for helping an individual become aware of the triggers that cause certain behaviors to surface, thus making it easier for them to self-regulate when those triggers arise.

Reflective Response. In contrast to the reactive response, the reflective response is conducive to learning. Reflective Response is evidenced by:

- *Calm body*
- *Focused mind*
- *Balanced emotions*

These states of being give way to better memory, both short-term and long-term, and better learning.

The goal of the Acting Right strategies is to keep students out of reactive response and in a reflective response mode.

The Acting Right strategies are grounded in age-old theatrical games. I have reshaped them to serve as effective tools for teaching behavior in the classroom, as well as to give teachers a behavior-based vocabulary to shape our conversations with our students. Acting Right helps you set the stage to use these games and vocabulary all day, every day. The ongoing use of the strategies gives them power.

As a final note, many teachers have told me they do not have time to teach behavior because they are pressured to cover the curriculum within a certain timeframe. I completely understand. But in response, I ask them to look at how much time they spend actually teaching a lesson compared to how much time they spend attempting to manage behavior. Sending a student to the office, stopping class to address off-task or disruptive behaviors, or using other managing methods eats time away from teaching.

If you invest the time to teach behavior, rather than attempt to manage it, you will be amazed at how much more time you will have for teaching. The investment in the Acting Right strategies will have a powerful and beneficial domino effect, impacting every moment and every interaction in your classroom. Taking the time to teach behavior will impact your class' concentration and cooperation, enabling your students to succeed not only in the classroom, but as they navigate throughout their lives.

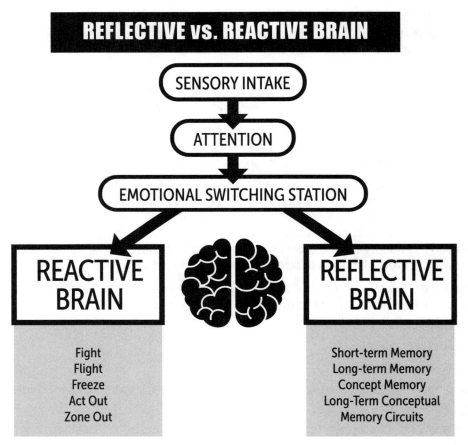

Figure 1 - 2006 Judy Willis, M.D., M. Ed. [4]

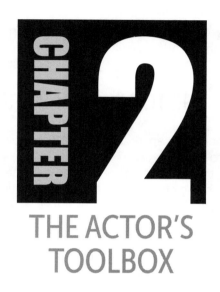

CHAPTER

2

THE ACTOR'S
TOOLBOX

"Our first question about children should not be 'How can we make them do what we want?'

but rather, 'What do they require in order to flourish, and how can we provide these things?'"

— Alfie Kohn

The Actor's Toolbox is the first of four Acting Right strategies.

1. *Actor's Toolbox*
2. *Cooperation Challenge*
3. *Concentration Circle*
4. *One-Minute Challenge Tableau*

Through the Actor's Toolbox, students demonstrate their agreement to control their bodies, voices, and minds, as well as to concentrate and cooperate.

THE TOOLBOX AS A "RESET" BUTTON

How do teachers prepare for students' widely varying energies and emotions that students bring to the classroom? Imagine this: It's early morning and the school gymnasium is buzzing with the arrival of students, some in the fog of a poor night's sleep, others still simmering after being chastised by a parent, and still others overstimulated by the presence of active peers. Soon this scattered, boisterous, rowdy group of students hurries off to their classrooms—and yours!

Wouldn't it be great if all the teacher had to do was push a reset button, and within a minute, without even having to speak, her class would be standing in front of her in a calm, focused, balanced state ready for any instruction? The first strategy in Acting Right gives teachers the gift of that reset button.

A silent routine, underscored with music, balances the energy of the group and readies them for learning. This is the Actor's Toolbox. Hundreds of teachers throughout the nation experience its power and use it on a daily basis as a reset button.

> A silent routine, underscored with music, balances the energy of the group and readies them for learning.

THE ELEMENTS OF ACTING

The foundations of the Acting Right strategies are theater exercises that have proven effective for generations of actors. They are active strategies that make students' readiness for learning readily apparent. In a traditional classroom setting, it can be challenging to determine if students are calm, focused, and balanced when they are sitting at desks and working independently. Students' ability to complete work isn't necessarily a good indicator of a mental state.

To make students' readiness for learning visible, each day, or class period, begins with the Actor's Toolbox, Acting Right's first strategy. My theatrical training taught me that an actor has a "toolbox" that includes three basic tools that contribute to an effective performance:

- **Body** – *Actors must use and/or change their bodies to move like the character they pretend to be. Actors must have control of their bodies.*

- **Voice** – *Actors must use and/or change their voices to speak like the character they pretend to be. Actors must have control of their voices.*

- **Imagination** – *Actors must be able to imagine that both the character and situation are real and stay focused throughout a performance. Actors must have control over their imagination and their focus to maintain the audience's attention.*

Additionally, there are two skills that actors use:

- **Cooperation** – *Usually, acting is not focused on one person. It requires interaction and cooperation. Actors must create relationships with their acting partners and be able to both speak and listen. For example, actors are aware of other actors' movements on stage and take turns saying their lines. In theatre working effectively is dependent on cooperation.*

- **Concentration** – *Concentration is key to actors' success in creating and maintaining their roles. It allows actors to remember their lines, movements, and other technical aspects of a scene. Concentration also helps actors cope with distractions such as another actor's mistake or disruptions from the audience. In theater, working effectively is dependent on concentration.*

Actors continually sharpen and refine their use of all five elements in the toolbox.

As you start to implement the Actor's Toolbox strategy in your classroom, you will see how these five elements reach beyond the realm of theater. Students' ability to control their body, voice, imagination, and their ability to cooperate and concentrate supports learning. The Acting Right goal is to develop students' capacity to self-regulate so they can achieve a calm, focused, and balanced state, not just as an individual, but as a group. As students become more proficient with the Actor's Toolbox, they will begin to work together effectively as a group, balance their energy for learning, and grow stronger in their ability to focus their attention without giving in to internal and external distractions.

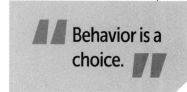
Behavior is a choice.

You will find that drama is not only an outlet for student expression; it is an effective way to teach behavior. All the Acting Right strategies are guided by this enduring understanding: Behavior is a choice.

Note that of the four Acting Right strategies, the Actor's Toolbox must be used first as it provides students with the important transition from a reactive to a reflective response in which they are in a calm, focused, and balanced state. Two Acting Right strategies—the Cooperation Challenge, and the Concentration Circle—follow the Actor's Toolbox and can be used in any order. The final Acting Right strategy, the One-Minute Challenge Tableau, must be used last.

In other words, always do the Actor's Toolbox first, then pair it with another strategy depending on the class' energy. For example, if the class is hyperactive, do the Cooperation Challenge so that your students can release that energy and focus. Or, if the class is calm, focused, and balanced, you can pair the Actor's Toolbox with the Concentration Circle. Use your discretion to determine whether an additional strategy would be effective.

THE ACTOR'S TOOLBOX: SCRIPT

"My students love the Actor's Toolbox. It's the moment of every day that just brings us together as a class. It's like what we do to say that we're now at school, this is my community, this is my team. It's kind of like our team huddle."

"The students sign their contract every single day. It's basically a contract that they're signing to promise me, promise themselves, and promise their classmates that they will concentrate, cooperate and control their body, voice, and imagination. And so I hold them to that contract throughout the day. Instead of saying "Stop talking" I can say, "What have you lost control of?" If at any time throughout the day my class is not calm, focused, or balanced, we sign the contract again just to bring the energy of that room back to my expectations for learning. At this point, the Actor's Toolbox is just part of our normal routine. My students have learned to have their energy calm, focused, and balanced, so at this stage of the game, they don't NEED to do the Actor's Toolbox procedure. But they LIKE to do it. Optimal learning happens when bodies are calm, minds are focused, and emotions are balanced. The energy of my room now is always that way. Anytime the energy is not calm, focused, or balanced in the classroom, it is a reminder to the student, a reminder to their classmates, and a reminder to me, that we should fix it."

— Carrie Chinners, fourth grade teacher

The Actor's Toolbox is a physical contract students "sign" to demonstrate their agreement to control their bodies, voices, and minds, as well as to concentrate and cooperate. To signal to students that they should silently form a circle to begin the activity, play the song InnerSpace by Nancy Krebs, available for download at www.ArtsIntegrationConsulting.com. Always use the same music, as students will associate the music with this exercise.

To introduce the Actor's Toolbox, use the following script. The words you will speak are in italics. You will use this script only to establish the procedure. Once established, you will lead the routine without speaking.

Begin with students seated in a circle.

SCRIPT: 📄 *THE ACTOR'S TOOLBOX*

STEP 1: Introduce Five Tools

We are about to have an actor's workout.

Actors don't work out these muscles [point to arms] *,*

or these muscles [point to legs] *.*

Actors work out these muscles [point to brain] *.*

To begin our workout, we need to know that an actor's job is to PRETEND. Actors pretend to be someone or something else. In order to do that, they use some tools—not tools like hammers and saws. Actors use tools like costumes, make-up, and the words they say, called scripts.

When we look in our Actor's Toolbox this year, we won't find those tools. We will find five that you bring to school with you every day.

*The first is your **body.***

*The second is your **voice**.*

*The third is your **imagination**.*

*The fourth is **concentration**.*

*The fifth is **cooperation**.*

So we have five tools: Body, voice, imagination, concentration, and cooperation.

I need you to remember all five tools. I will show you an easy way to remember. We put the words in our bodies, just like this.

Watch me first, and then you get to try.

STEP 2: Demonstrate Body

[Stand up and demonstrate. Make sure students are watching and not doing.]

We will begin by standing up and imagining our bodies are a building.

We will bend over and touch our toes, imagining our fingers are in the basement of the building—in an elevator. The elevator goes up.

[Slowly stand up, keep your fingers in contact with the sides of your body.]

*This reminds us that actors use their **bodies**.*

STEP 3: Demonstrate Voice

[Continue raising your fingers and when they reach your throat, stop.]

*The elevator stops at this floor, reminding us that actors use their **voices.***

Take a deep breath and hold it. Make a small sound with your voice when you let it out. [Demonstrate.]

STEP 4: Demonstrate Imagination

[Move your fingers up your body until you reach your temples.]

*The elevator keeps moving up and stops at the next floor. This reminds us that actors use their **imaginations**.*

Close your eyes and—without using your voice or your body— take a field trip anywhere in the universe using your imagination. Go somewhere that makes you happy. I am going to a beach. I will be right back.

[Close your eyes. Pause for 10 seconds. Open your eyes.]

Come back by opening your eyes.

STEP 5: Demonstrate Concentration & Cooperation

[Place hands beside your eyes.]

*Now place your hands on either side of your eyes, blocking out every- thing beside you. Zoom your focus in on one thing in front of you. Stretch out your hands to keep your focus on that one thing. This shows that actors **concentrate**.*

*Now raise your hands up, then bring them down, and put them on the person's back or shoulder on either side of you. This reminds us that actors **cooperate**.*

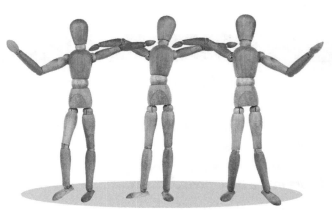

STEP 6: Demonstrate Entire Toolbox

The whole thing looks like this. Watch.

[Silently demonstrate the Toolbox starting at body, then throat, temples, and eyes. Stretch arms out to focus, then raise your hands up and then lower them to place them on the person's back or shoulder on either side of you.]

It's not a race. We will do it together, at the same time.

STEP 7: Students Demonstrate

Now you are ready to try! Stand up and let's start from the beginning.

[Guide students to do these actions with you. Students might laugh, joke, and sabotage during this step. Let it happen. Observe.]

Bend over and put your fingers in the basement of the building.

The elevator goes up. This reminds us that actors use their... [prompt students to fill in] ***bodies***.

Stop at your throat. This reminds us that actors use their... [prompt students to fill in] ***voices***.

Take a deep breath. Hold it. And make a small sound as you let it out.

Keep moving up the elevator and stop here. [Gesture towards temples.]

Actors use their... [prompt students to fill in] ***imaginations***.

Close your eyes and use your imagination to go anywhere you want—back home, to grandma's house, to another state, another planet—somewhere that makes you happy.

Your eyes should be closed and your voices silent. [pause]

Come back by opening your eyes.

Now place your hands on either side of your eyes blocking out everything beside you. Stretch out your hands to lock your focus on one thing.

This shows that actors ... [prompt students to fill in] ***concentrate***.

Now raise your hands up, bring them down, and put them on the person's back or shoulder on either side of you.

This reminds us that actors ... [prompt students to fill in] ***cooperate***.

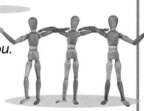

STEP 8: Repeat with Music and without Words

Put your arms down and let's try it again.

This time, I won't talk and you won't talk. I will put some music on and we will move our bodies the same way.

Even though no one is talking, you are saying a lot to me! It's like you are speaking in sign language to me.

Here is what you are saying when you move your body this way:

- [Move arms up your body] *"Today I agree to control my* **body***."*

- [Place hands at your throat] *When we do this, we are really saying, "Today I agree to control my* **voice***."*

- [Place hands at your temples] *"And my... **imagination**."*

- [Place hands on either side of your eyes, and raise arms to place on those next to you]

"Today I will **concentrate** *and* **cooperate***."*

This is now a contract you are signing, an agreement you are making. We don't need pens and paper. We have your bodies.

I will know you are signing the contract because you do this: [Make first gesture in the sequence, BODY.]

I will know you are NOT signing the contract if ...

We are all doing this with our bodies [show correct BODY gesture] and you are wiggling around, touching your neighbor, or NOT doing it. [You can add some behaviors you saw happen in Step Eight.]

This would be your way telling me that today you are choosing NOT to control your body.

I will know you are NOT signing the contract if ...

We are all doing this with our bodies [show VOICE gesture] and you are laughing or talking or whispering with your neighbor. This is your way of telling me that today you are choosing NOT to control your voice.

I will know you are NOT signing the contract if ...

We are all doing this with our bodies [show COOPERATION gesture] and you make a nasty face when you put your hands on the shoulder of the person beside you, or if you are not touching them, or [add some behaviors you observed in Step 8].

This is your way of telling me that today you are choosing NOT to cooperate.

If you make the weak choice not to use or control one of your actor tools or skills, I will ask you to return to your seat and you can watch what the rest of us—who are strong enough to bring all five tools to class—do with them.

You can watch until you are strong enough to bring the missing tool or tools back to our group.

I will put the music on, you will move your bodies, and I will see who agrees to that contract! Here we go.

[Play music and have students do Actor's Toolbox together with you.]

[Carefully observe. If a student does not complete a step the way you demonstrated, stop, tell students what you observed, and repeat, giving the student an opportunity to correct the behavior. Build positive peer pressure. Say, "Even though most of you are agreeing to control your voices (or other tool), I can tell some students are not controlling their voices because I hear them talking (or other unwanted behavior). Let's start again so that I can see if those students can make a stronger choice." Repeat three times before asking the student to return to their desk.]

STEP 9: Introduce Calm, Focused & Balanced

Let's try one more time and this time I will be watching for three new things – CALM, FOCUS, AND BALANCE.

Let me explain.

- *Calm is about your body. Because you could sign the contract like this:* **[Demonstrate with a wiggly body.]** *That is not calm. THIS is calm:* **[Demonstrate with a relaxed body.]**

- *Focus is about your mind. Because you could sign the contract like this:* **[Demonstrate by looking all around at everyone in the circle.]** *That is not focused. THIS is focused:* **[Demonstrate by looking straight ahead.]**

- *Balance is not about the outside of your body. It is about the inside – your emotions. Because you could sign the contract like this:* **[Demonstrate with smiling and laughter.]** *That is not balanced. THIS is balanced:* **[Demonstrate with neutral facial expression.]**

Let's try again and see who is strong enough to bring calm, focus, and balance to our team.

[Repeat Actor's Toolbox.]

[Carefully observe, even more than before. If a student does not complete each step of the procedure in a calm, focused, and balanced way, stop immediately, tell the students what you observed, and have the entire class repeat. Build positive peer pressure. Repeat only three times for one student who is not complying before asking that student to sit out.]

STEP 10: Reflect

Sit down in the circle for a moment. I have a couple of questions for you.

We will do this Actor's Toolbox every day. There are so many things we are supposed to be learning, and yet, we will take the time to do THIS every day. Why? How will doing this help your brain learn?

[Take some responses.]

I have another question for you. When you hear the fire alarm sound, it tells your brain to do some things and not do some things. Let's talk about those. When you hear the fire alarm, what are the things that your brain will tell you to do?

[Take some responses. Line up, walk out, etc.]

When you hear the fire alarm, what does it tell your brain NOT to do?

[Take some responses. Don't run, don't scream, etc.]

The music I just played for the Actor's Toolbox is going to be like a fire drill. When you hear it, it will tell your brain to DO some things, and NOT do some things. Let's talk about those.

When you hear that song, it will tell your brain to STOP what you are doing and find calm body, focused mind, and balanced emotions. You will walk over to this open space and make a standing circle. Once everyone is here, you will "sign the contract."

The music will NOT tell your brain to run, talk, or touch anyone. The music will NOT tell your brain you need to come back to the SAME place in the circle each time. And the music will NOT ask you to tell anyone with words or gestures what to do.

STEP 11: Practice Procedure

We are going to try it. When I say "go" you can go anywhere in the room you normally can go. You can talk with your friends, you can read a book, you can do some work at your desk. After a minute, I will play the music. When you hear it, what are you going to do?

[Ask a few students until they have listed the entire procedure.]

Those are the things you will do. What about the things you will NOT do? What are you NOT going to do?

[Ask a few students until they have listed several of the things you talked about.]

Now that we have talked about what it will look like, and what it won't look like, how many times do you think it will take before it looks the way we want it to look? Hold up your fingers. Show me a quick prediction.

Let's give it a try! Go!

[Students move around room and begin talking, etc. Let the energy rise before playing music. Once you play the music, watch for behaviors. Have students repeat the procedure until there is 100% accuracy. It typically can take 3-5 times before enough positive peer pressure—other students telling each other the behavior is unacceptable or displaying frustrated energy—is created for the behaviors to change.]

Note that this script is for use only the first time the activity is introduced. Every subsequent time the Actor's Toolbox is used, simply put on the music, make a circle, and ask the students to show you that they remember and agree to the tools that you will be using today. Otherwise, there should be no talking on the teacher's part. As the students become accustomed to the activity, it will require only 10 to 30 seconds to complete.

IMPLICATIONS OF THE USE OF THE ACTOR'S TOOLBOX

Because its purpose is to balance the group's energy, the Actor's Toolbox is not only a transition activity but a "reset button." It resets students' energies and aligns the group into a calm, focused, and balanced state.

You must wonder how often you will need to push the "reset button." I suggest using this activity first thing in the morning to reset whatever energy students bring from home. Then I would apply it every time all your students return to the classroom (e.g., from lunch, from recess). This allows you to reset the energy and re-establish your leadership.

Gradually, your students will come to associate your classroom environment with that calm, focused, and balanced energy, and you will not need to use the Actor's Toolbox as frequently. When they internalize the process, they will begin to self-regulate their behavior without the music trigger and without physically signing the contract. In a sense, this process is Pavlovian in nature. You are training your students to associate the music, and your classroom environment.

Remember to assess behavior during the Actor's Toolbox routine. If you see behavior that is inconsistent with the activity's expectations, stop and say,

"Even though most of you are agreeing to control your voices (or other tool), I can tell some students are not controlling their voices because I see them talking (or other unwanted behavior). Let's start again so that I can see if those students can make a stronger choice."

OBSERVE 🔍 FOR THESE UNWANTED/CONCERNING BEHAVIORS		
Laughing/smiling	Sighing	Not touching shoulders at the end of the routine
Darting eyes	Eye rolling	Squeezing neighbor's shoulders at end of routine
Talking	Lethargic movements	Head down to avoid eye contact

CHANGING OUR VOCABULARY

The vocabulary you will need to teach behavior is established through the Actor's Toolbox.

There is a large body of scholarly work about the power of language in teaching[5]. Studies consistently show the impact of language subtleties on students[6]. Personally, I have found a strong correlation between the words I use and the behavior I see.

Acting Right uses two adjectives to describe a student's behavioral choices: strong and weak. Most behavior we do not want is a student's quest for power in front of their peers. Some students feel their peers admire them when they challenge the teacher by showing defiance, or breaking a rule. They gain a perceived power by misbehaving. If we accept that premise, then calling a behavior "bad" or "wrong" is counterproductive. In many communities, the word "bad" = strong and the word "wrong" = strong. By labeling behavior with those terms, the teacher inadvertently empowers the student.

Instead, let's switch the paradigm and put semantics on our side. If students' misbehavior is a quest for power and we label their behavioral choice as "weak," it makes it difficult for the students to continue making that choice if they want to be perceived as powerful. Likewise, if we label a behavioral choice as "strong," it makes it much more empowering for students to choose or repeat that behavior.

Teachers may initially feel uncomfortable using these adjectives. Let me be clear: the adjectives are used to describe CHOICES not the PERSON. I do not say, "Sam, you are being weak for talking." That is a personal attack on Sam and will most likely send him into a reactive mode. Instead, I say, "Sam, I am confused at the weak choice you are making to talk while I am talking." This language puts the focus on the choice and not the person. Follow the statement with a challenge to make a stronger choice. "Sam, can you make the stronger choice to control your voice?"

Another example: "Sam, I am confused at the WEAK choice you are making to talk while I am talking. Will you help the team by making the STRONGER choice to control your voice?" This statement makes it difficult for Sam to continue to make a weak choice when his peers are aware that there is a strong choice.

I suggest you further reframe your vocabulary by using the vocabulary the Actor's Toolbox provides as your guide *(see table on next page)*. For example:

- *Instead of saying "Be quiet," say "Show that you are in control of your voice."*
- *Instead of saying "Calm down," say "Show that you are in control of your body."*

If one or more students continue to demonstrate a lack of control of one of the tools, ask them to return to their seats until they are "strong" enough to bring all the tools back to the group.

Please note that the Actor's Toolbox should not be used as a tool for punishing unwanted behavior, such as when a student interrupts you during class. One student's inappropriate response does not require "a reset." The class should not engage again in the procedure. If a student interrupts, simply address the behavior with a correction such as "We agreed that we would control our bodies. Please show that you can honor that agreement. Are you ready now to make a STRONGER choice to control your body and your voice?"

Remember, behavior is a literacy and like any literacy, practice is important to mastering it. With the Actor's Toolbox, you are teaching behavior, not managing it. That distinction is critical. As students internalize the lessons of the Actor's Toolbox, you will have successfully taught them to be calm, focused, and balanced—and ready for learning.

The Actor's Toolbox is strongest when you follow it with the other Acting Right strategies, allowing the Actor's Toolbox to be the doorway to the other engaging strategies described in the following chapters.

> **Remember, behavior is a literacy and like any literacy, practice is important to mastering it. With the Actor's Toolbox, you are teaching behavior, not managing it. That distinction is critical.**

BENEFITS OF THE ACTOR'S TOOLBOX

The Actor's Toolbox has multiple benefits in the classroom environment, including:

- *Enables "Reflective Brain"*
- *Diffuses the "Reactive Brain"*
- *Provides a kinesthetic review and/or agreement of tools, elements, rules/expectations*
- *Establishes a vocabulary for self-regulation/control*
- *Helps both teachers and students assess behavior*
- *Provides a clear, unifying transition that balances the group's energy*
- *Provides a framework for reflection*
- *Supports and builds on Bodily/Kinesthetic and Intrapersonal Intelligences*

THE ACTING RIGHT VOCABULARY

The Acting Right strategies use a particular vocabulary to help students make positive behavioral choices and to give them feedback on their choices. Use the Actor's Toolbox vocabulary throughout the day, even when you are not using the strategies.

THE OLD WAY: **VOICE**	THE NEW WAY: **VOICE**
Be quiet. *Stop talking.* *Shhhh!*	"Show that you are in control of your voice."
	"Is that talking helping or hurting the team?" (Student answers: hurting.) "Show that you can make the stronger choice to help instead of hurt."
	Which tool am I about to ask you to control?" (Student responds.) "How do we know you have lost control?" (Student responds.) "Show us that you can make the stronger choice."
	"I'm confused. Everyone else is making the strong choice to control their voices right now, but you are not. Please help us by making that same strong choice."
	"I am surprised you are making such a weak choice with your voice. Are you strong enough to make the choice all other [5th graders] are making? Show us."

THE OLD WAY: **BODY**	THE NEW WAY: **BODY**
Get up. *Stop touching.* *Calm down.*	"Show that you are in control of your body."
	"Is that energy helping or hurting the team right now?" (Student answers: hurting.) "Show that you can make the stronger choice to help instead of hurt."
	(Place hand on student's shoulder and speak softly) "Calm energy."
	"Which tool am I about to ask you to control?" (Student responds.) "How do we know you have lost control?" (Student responds.) "Show us that you can make the stronger choice."
	"I'm confused. Everyone else is making the strong choice to control their bodies right now, and you are not. Please help us by making that same strong choice."
	"I am surprised you are making such a weak choice with your body. Are you strong enough to make the choice all other [5th graders] are making? Please help us by making that same strong choice."

REFLECTION QUESTIONS FOR STUDENTS

Taking time to reflect with students after engaging in the Actor's Toolbox is critical in helping them make sense of and learn from their experience. The following questions invite students to consider their feelings and thoughts about the Actor's Toolbox as well as transform their thinking.

Feel

How does it feel when we do the Actor's Toolbox together?

Think

What are you saying to me when you participate in the Actor's Toolbox?

What can we do, while we are signing the contract, to help someone who is making weak choices?

What does it tell you if we all are not strong enough to sign the contract?

Transform

How does the Actor's Toolbox help you?

How do you think the Actor's Toolbox helps me—as your teacher?

How could the Actor's Toolbox help you throughout the day?
Ten years from now?

COMMON PITFALLS IN FACILITATION

My experience providing instructional coaching to teachers leading the Actor's Toolbox has helped me uncover the following common pitfalls that are typically made when learning how to facilitate this strategy:

Teacher talks too much – The power of using drama is that it is active. Do not turn this activity into a lecture. Get to the "doing" part as quickly as possible. It is only the first time you introduce the activity that you need to use the script. After the initial experience, talking will not be necessary.

Lack of assessment – One of the main objectives in using this activity is for the students to show you (without words) that they understand and agree to use the tools and skills necessary. If they are talking or not taking the activity seriously, you must restart it.

Assertive, serious approach – Teacher's tone must communicate that the Actor's Toolbox is important and valuable. An assertive and serious and approach must be established and maintained if you want students to accept the procedure's value.

Misusing as a management tool – This activity should not be used as a tool for punishing unwanted behavior and repeated every time an unwanted behavior occurs. When these situations surface, simply address the behavior with a correction.

FREQUENTLY ASKED QUESTIONS

In leading professional development workshops for teachers, the following questions typically arise regarding the use and facilitation of the Actor's Toolbox:

How long should it take to lead the Actor's Toolbox?

It should take no longer than five to ten minutes to initially teach the routine. After that, it takes 10 to 30 seconds to perform the activity, depending on student behavior. Just put the music on and do it!

How often should I use this?

At the beginning of the year, you should use the Actor's Toolbox routine every day and continue to do so for at least a month. Eventually, you will need it only for select moments throughout the year. (Note: Many students ask to participate in this daily, as it helps them transition to the classroom.) Throughout each day of the year, however, it is important to continue to use the vocabulary for controlling the voice, body, imagination, concentration, and cooperation.

Why do I have to use the music?

The music becomes a signal or prompt that communicates the routine is starting. Playing the music replaces the teacher's need to say, "Everyone come over here and let's do the Actor's Toolbox!" The music also plays a big part in leveling the energy of the class and helping students make the transition.

Why do we have to make a circle?

There is something unifying about a circle. Making a circle reinforces the team-building aspect that you are trying to develop and foster within your class. A circle also prompts students to make eye contact with each other. Early in the year, the circle helps behaviors to surface, allowing you to see how much behavior reshaping is needed. I strongly suggest you make the space in your classroom that allows your students to create the circle.

Will the students really do this?

Yes! Elementary school students are eager to participate. You can expect more skepticism in middle and high school students. However, if you keep your tone calm, assertive, and matter of fact, it will work. Tell the students this is a physical contract that they need to sign before you begin class.

HELPING STUDENTS REFLECT ON THEIR BEHAVIOR

The following form can be used with students to help them reflect on their behavioral choices:

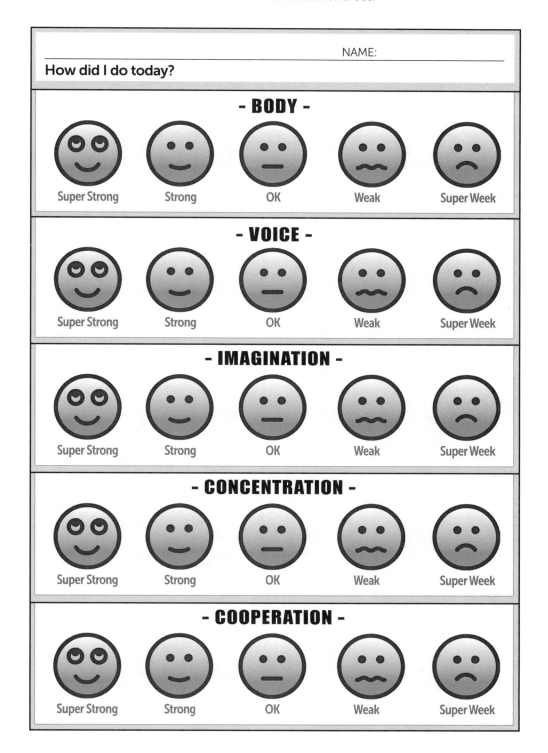

NAME: _____

Next time, I will work more on: *(circle one)*

BODY   VOICE   IMAGINATION   CONCENTRATION   COOPERATION

I need to work more on this because...

3 things I learned about cooperation today were:

1.

2.

3.

3 things I learned about myself today were:

1.

2.

3.

THE CONCENTRATION CIRCLE

"Concentration is the secret of strength."

— Ralph Waldo Emerson

CULTIVATING CONCENTRATION FOR LEARNING

Schools can be busy, bustling, and even distracting places. Students are coming and going, chatting with peers, sharpening pencils, getting supplies, and asking questions. Announcements are made over the intercom, bells are ringing, and sounds from the playground fill the air. Those are merely some of the external distractions. Internally, students' thoughts can race around and center on a scores of things other than schoolwork. We expect these students to concentrate although we have never taught them how to do it.

Drama gives us an ideal context for developing concentration skills. Consider an actor on the stage. Weeks or months of work have prepared the actor for what she will say, when she will say it, how she will say it, and where she will move on stage as she says it. Candy wrappers may crackle in the audience, another actor may forget a line, a stagehand may drop something backstage, but good actors stay focused and remain in the moment to give an effective performance. For actors, concentration on stage is a skill that they develop through hard work and practice.

Students do not arrive in our classrooms with full command of their ability to concentrate and focus. We must cultivate those skills. As stated earlier, behavior is a literacy, and as with any literacy, it must be taught. And like a muscle, concentration does not grow strong if it is not exercised consistently.

> **Students must develop a filter for their impulses and..."be the boss" of their brain.**

We know that the ability to concentrate is a critical skill for effective learning. It determines whether students will be able to persevere through challenging tasks. It dictates whether students will be able to stay focused on a task long enough to build their understandings and complete the work. If our students do not learn to shut out distractions, they will struggle to succeed both in the classroom and in life.

Psychologist Daniel Goleman, author of *Focus: The Hidden Driver of Excellence*, maintains that the circuitry of the brain requires sustained stretches of concentration[7] to enable learning. Goleman suggests that educators must become more intentional about teaching the skills of focus and concentration.

Again, I'll point out that it is more effective to teach concentration rather than manage distracted behavior.

A Virginia Commonwealth University research paper published in 2011 asserted that there is a direct connection between concentration and self-regulation. Students must be able to concentrate and control their focus by clearing their minds of distracting thoughts. This is linked to the ability to self-regulate; the ability to manage one's thoughts, emotions, and behaviors[8]. Students must develop a filter for their impulses and, as we say in Acting Right, they must "be the boss" of their brain.

THE CONCENTRATION CIRCLE: SCRIPT

"Acting Right strategies harness the power of social learning. The Concentration Circle is an empowerment strategy that helps students realize that they can control their attention, ignore distractions, and challenge their initial reactions by "talking back" to their brains.

"Teaching students that they're in charge of their concentration is critical. In many classrooms, students blame other classmates or other things for their behavior. 'I can't read because he's talking' or 'I didn't do my math because of the noise.' However, with the Concentration Circle students are empowered and know that they can to choose how they respond to external stimuli. They know behavior is a choice."
– Melanie Rick, national Acting Right consultant

"Students hear 'concentrate, concentrate' all the time, but they don't know what that means. The Concentration Circle teaches them what that means. And its effective! So now we play The Concentration Circle more as a reminder than a necessity. They're so in tune now with themselves that they might even say " Ms. Chinners, can we play a few levels of concentration because we need it."
– Carrie Chinners, fourth grade teacher

"The Concentration Circle provides students with a space and an opportunity that they don't usually have—quietness of that time and the challenge of the teacher trying to distract them. What I see is when students complete that type of practice, they are able to attend to their reading and their math in a much more focused way."
– Winston Cox, principal

The next Acting Right strategy, the Concentration Circle, is a great workout for the concentration "muscle."

For this activity, you will need some unique objects—Jewels of Concentration. As magical as it sounds, Jewels of Concentration are nothing more than decorative plastic "diamonds." During the following exercise, each student receives a "jewel" to represent their concentration. If students are successful at maintaining their concentration during this activity, they keep the "jewel;" if they are not successful, they lose their concentration and literally must give up the jewel.

Jewels of Concentration are a strategic learning tool because they make an abstract concept, such as concentration, concrete. We cannot see concentration, hear it, or touch it. When teaching an abstract concept, best practice suggests we create a visible metaphor – something you can see, hear, and touch. The jewels make this intangible concept of concentration, tangible. I discourage the use of other objects such as a penny or a piece of candy, as those do not establish a strong metaphor for concentration. The object must be precious and valuable. Because students typically find the jewels alluring, they grasp the concept that the jewel, and by transference, their concentration, is something of value that they don't want to lose. It is an effective strategy, used until students internalize the concept.

Keep in mind that your role during the Concentration Circle is to coach (help students who lose their concentration find a way to regain it), monitor (pay attention to what the student leader is doing), and serve as a commentator (give the class updates such as, "No one has lost their jewel yet.").

To introduce this activity, use the following script. Once again, the words you will speak are in italics. Complete the Actor's Toolbox first, then continue to play the music and begin this activity with students standing in a circle.

SCRIPT: 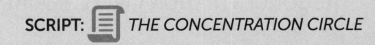 *THE CONCENTRATION CIRCLE*

PREPARATION: The Concentration Circle

Let's see how strong your concentration muscles are.

They are not here. [Point to arms]

They are not here. [Point to legs]

They are HERE. [Point to brain]

You will have to SHOW me how strong your concentration muscles are. Here is how you will do it.

Everyone can see a wall somewhere in front of you. No one has to turn around to see a wall.

With your eyes, find one spot on that wall to stare at. This spot will not move. Do not choose a spot on a person, or the hands of the clock, or a bird on a branch outside, because these will move.

This spot on the wall will be called your focal point, because it is the point that is getting all of your focus and all of your attention.

My focal point is going to be. [Tell class what point you will stare at]

You should be able to SAY the name of your focal point.

Find a point on the wall in front of you.

I don't have time to hear what focal point EACH of you have chosen, so for now, just point to yours.

[Make sure everyone is pointing straight ahead.]

Let me check in with a few of you.

[Ask a few students, whose ability to concentrate may be questionable, to name their focal point.]

What is YOUR focal point? [If their focal point can't be identified or is too broad, identify one for the student.]

If your concentration muscles are strong, you should be able to keep your eyes locked on that focal point for up to a minute.

You can blink and you can breathe. You should do both.

But you are not looking around the circle laughing, smiling, or talking.

Before we begin to play the Concentration Game, take your eyes OFF of your focal point and make ME your focal point.

[Make sure all students are looking at you.]

Great! Everyone understands what I mean. Our focal point can change. It does all day long.

Make your shoes your focal point. Make the ceiling your focal point. Make your neighbor your focal point. Make the clock your focal point. Make your tongue your focal point. Make ME your focal point.

Here is how we will play.

BODY: Neutral Position

You will put your body in neutral position—that means standing, arms by your side, and your eyes are on a focal point.

Your arms are not crossed in front you or behind your back. Your hands are not in your pockets or on your hips. Your body is straight, arms by your side, eyes on your focal point—neutral position—and I start the timer for one whole minute.

But here is what is going to happen...

MIND: Talking Back to Your Brain

As you stand there, your brain is going to start sending you messages. Messages like:

> **Move your hands.**
> **Scratch your cheek.**
> **Lick your lips.**
> **Look around.**
> **Smile.**
> **Fix your shirt.**
> **Shift your weight.**

There are so many messages your brain might send.

What will you say to your brain when it says those things?
[Students should respond: No!]

Concentration is a conversation you have with your brain where YOU become the boss of your brain.

Who thinks they are strong enough to be the boss of their brain?

We'll find out.

LEVEL 1: Maintaining Focus

Body is in neutral position, eyes on your focal point. Here we go.

[As students stand, remind them to stay frozen. If students take their eyes off their focal point, smile, laugh, or move out of neutral position, with warmth encourage them to re-focus. Make the student aware they are not focused—re-focus the student—and continue.]

[Say things like: "If your hands are moving, you are NOT the boss of your brain." "If you are scratching your face, you are NOT the boss of your brain."]

[Continue about a minute, but don't be exact. You are gauging their capacity more than strictly watching the clock.]

[When you are finished, say:]

Time is up. Take your eyes off of your focal point. Laugh, smile, talk to your neighbors for three seconds. Go! [Students respond.]

Now make ME your focal point. This is like a video game. There is level one, two, three, four, five, and six. Each level gets more challenging. THAT was level one. If ONE person looks, laughs, smiles, or talks, we ALL stay at level one until everyone is strong enough to move up to the next level together.

[Repeat Level 1 if necessary. If not, proceed to Level 2.]

[NOTE: This activity may be very difficult for your class or for an individual. Remember not to treat the loss of concentration as a disruption or disobedience; it is merely a sign that the concentration "muscle" is weak and needs this exercise. Constantly encourage students not to lose their focus just because another student has lost theirs.]

MATERIALS REQUIRED: Jewels of Concentration

Let's move on to Level 2.

Before we begin, it will help if you imagine that your concentration, which is really somewhere in your brain, is really here—in your hand.

[Hold out hand like you are holding something.]

It is something you can really hold on to. It will also help to think of your concentration as something that is valuable—something you would not want to lose. Something you probably would not want to lose is a diamond or a jewel.

So let's imagine, in your hand, is a jewel of concentration. Hold it out in front of you. [Pretend to hold a jewel in your hand.]

Some people are strong enough to hold on to their jewel of concentration. In this game, that means they keep their body in neutral position and their eyes on a focal point.

Other people move, wiggle, scratch, laugh, or look around, and what happens to their jewel? They lose it. [Pretend to drop jewel.]

In this game, I need to see who is strong enough to hold onto their concentration, and whose muscles are weak and will cause them to lose their jewel.

To help us keep track of that, I have a real bag of Jewels of Concentration. I want to show you what one of the jewels looks like.

[Take out a Jewel of Concentration and hold it in your hand.]

They all look the same.

I am coming around and putting one in YOUR hand.

When I do, if you REALLY can't hold onto the jewel of concentration because you are so busy playing around with it and you drop it on the ground—even if it is an accident—it will come back to me.

If you put it in your mouth or nose, it will come back to me.

If you throw it up in the air or trade it with your neighbors, it will come back to me.

Let's see who is strong enough to REALLY hold onto their jewel.

As I walk around the circle and pass these out, your eyes do not need to be on your focal point. Take a minute to look at your jewel. Once everyone has one, we will begin.

[Distribute jewels.]

Is this REALLY your concentration? [Students should respond: No.]

Is this magic? Will it MAKE you concentrate? [Students should respond: No.]

Why do we have these in our hands? [Students should respond: To remind us to hold on to our concentration.]

LEVEL 2: Adult Distraction

Here's how we play level two.

You put your body in neutral position. You lock your eyes on a focal point.

I walk around in front of you and look you in your eyes.

If your concentration muscles are strong, you won't look back, laugh, or smile. If your brain tells you to look at me, what will you say back? [Students should respond: No!]

I hope so.

If you do look, laugh, smile, move, talk, I will just come by and take the jewel out of your hand.

Are you in trouble? [Students should respond: No.]

Why did I take it? You lost your concentration.

How will you get it back? [Students should respond: By concentrating.]

Right. If I look at you again and you are concentrating, I will come back and return the jewel to your hand.

Let's give it a try.

[Begin to walk around the circle and look each student in the eye. Do not talk to them or make any sounds.]

As I walk around the circle, I am looking behind me to make sure your eyes are on your focal point. I am also looking ahead of me to make sure your eyes are on your focal point.

Your eyes stay locked on that point the entire time, not just when I am in front of you. I will let you know when I am finished walking around the circle.

[If students take their eyes off their focal point, smile, laugh, or move out of neutral position, stop and encourage them to re-focus and/or take their jewel. Back up and pass in front of the students again to give them another chance to demonstrate their abilities to concentrate. When you are finished, say:]

I am finished. Take your eyes off of your focal point. Laugh, smile, talk to your neighbors for three seconds. Go! [Students respond.]

ENCOURAGING A CLASS TO PROGRESS TO THE NEXT LEVEL

Remind students that there are more challenging levels of this game, but they cannot progress until they master the current level. Do not tell them what the next level includes. Their curiosity and the challenge will motivate them to master the current level.

If some students lose their concentration during the activity, remember to take away their jewels. Their desire to keep the jewel will motivate them to build their concentration muscle. At the end of each round, however, return all collected jewels and begin again. Taking the jewel is only a tangible reminder that they have lost their concentration in that moment; it is not a punishment.

LEVEL 3: Peer Distraction

- *Instead of walking around the circle yourself, select someone from the class to walk around the circle, looking each student in the eye.*

- *There can be great excitement over who is selected to be the leader. Some students are more challenging leaders than others. Once a leader is selected, give the students a few seconds to laugh or smile before locking on their focal point.*

- *Remind the leader that he or she cannot talk, make any sounds, or touch the students. Also tell the leader that YOU are the judge and will collect the jewels if necessary.*

LEVEL 4: Visual Distraction

- *Pick a student to walk around the circle. The leader remains silent, but tries to steal participants' concentration by making funny and crazy faces.*

- *The leader is prohibited from making of any sounds.*

- *Remind students that they are still participating in the activity BEFORE and AFTER the leader looks at them. They must continue to stare at their focal point and maintain their concentration until the leader reaches the end of the circle.*

LEVEL 5: Visual & Sound Distractions

- *Select a student to walk around the circle. This time, however, the leader does not have to be silent! To try and steal participants' concentration, the leader will make crazy, funny faces and sounds.*

- *The leader cannot say words—only sounds. The sounds cannot be sounds that produce spit.*

- *Remind students that they are still participating in the activity BEFORE and AFTER the leader looks at them. They must continue to stare at their focal point and maintain their concentration until the leader reaches the end of the circle.*

LEVEL 6: Look, Listen & Speak!

This level provides an opportunity for students to maintain their concentration while they respond to a request.

The class begins standing a circle. One student is designated "It." "It's" objective is to cause another student to break his/her concentration and smile. "It" walks around the inside of the circle, picks a student and asks, "Won't you please smile?" Without smiling, the student must say, "I will not smile." "It" must continue to attempt to make the student smile using funny, crazy character voices or gestures. If the student loses concentration and smiles, that student becomes "It." If "It" does not convince a person to smile, he/she must approach another student in an attempt to break that student's concentration and cause him/her to smile.

If "It" cannot cause three consecutive students to smile, then someone volunteers to trade places and becomes "It." If this happens for three consecutive students playing "It"—meaning nine consecutive students do not smile—then the game is over. If, however, someone smiles, the count is reset to zero and the team works again towards achieving nine concentration successes in a row.

Students will ask what happens after Level 6. Tell them that REAL LIFE happens, and their challenge is to maintain focus in everyday situations.

REFLECTION QUESTIONS FOR STUDENTS

Taking time to reflect with students after engaging in the Concentration Circle is critical in helping them make sense of and learn from their experience. The following questions invite students to consider their feelings and thoughts about the Concentration Circle as well as transform their thinking.

Feel

What does it feel like to concentrate?

Think

What is challenging about this activity?

What are some things your brain is telling you to do instead of focus?

What are some strategies we can use to help us hold onto our concentration?

What do you think happens after Level 6?

Transform

How will this "game" help you at other times of the day? At home? In life?

COMMON PITFALLS IN FACILITATION

My experience providing instructional coaching to teachers leading the Concentration Circle has helped me uncover the following common pitfalls that are typically made when learning how to facilitate this strategy:

Lack of teacher in role of encourager – When students lose focus in this activity, do not treat is as a discipline issue but rather as a sign of weak concentration skills. Keep a neutral tone and work to empower each student to improve. Remember you are doing this to teach the skill.

Lack of assessment and moving to the next level too early – The objective of this activity is not to move to the next level as quickly as possible, but to make sure the class has mastered each level before moving on. Boredom is a good sign that the class is about to achieve the goal and to move to the next level!

FREQUENTLY ASKED QUESTIONS

In leading professional development workshops for teachers the following questions typically arise regarding the use and facilitation of the Concentration Circle:

How often should I use this?

At the beginning of the year, I would use the Concentration Circle every day and continue to use it until the class masters Level 6. Once they have made it that far, it is not necessary to use it anymore. There may be moments throughout the year, however, when touch-up or maintenance rounds are necessary. In any case, continue to use the vocabulary of focus and concentration throughout each day of the year.

What do I do while the student leader is walking around the circle?

You are facilitating. Follow the student leader and make sure they are not walking too slowly or too quickly. You are the judge as to whether someone loses a jewel, not the student leader. You are also giving commentary such as, "The leader is halfway around the circle," "Four people have lost their jewels," or, "There are only three more people left." And finally, you are coaching students who have weak concentration muscles with encouraging words such as "You can do this! You have already done it for 20 seconds, just go 10 more seconds!" or "It is okay that you lost your concentration, now get it back. I know you can!"

What happens if a student laughs and loses their jewel?

You have a choice based on the students and the moment. Either coach the students to success and let them keep the jewel, or take it away. If you take the jewel, return it to them when the student leader is finished with the round. You take the jewel only to remind the students that they lost their concentration. The jewel is used this way as a reminder and not as a disciplinary tool.

BENEFITS OF THE CONCENTRATION CIRCLE

The Concentration Circle has multiple benefits in the classroom environment, such as:

- *Introducing and reinforcing concentration as a skill that can be developed*
- *Harnessing and stabilizing group energy*
- *Establishing a vocabulary for focus*
- *Empowering the individual*
- *Enabling teacher assessment*
- *Facilitating intrapersonal intelligence*

THE ACTING RIGHT Az VOCABULARY

The following vocabulary can be established when the Concentration Circle has been introduced:

THE OLD WAY	THE NEW WAY
Pay Attention	"Make [X] your focal point."

THE OLD WAY: **BODY**	THE NEW WAY: **BODY**
Focus *All eyes on me*	What should your focal point be right now?" (Student responds) "Show me." "How do I know you have lost your focus?" (Student responds) "Please make a stronger choice." "I'm confused. Everyone else is making the strong choice to focus right now, and you are not. Please help us." "I am surprised you are making such a weak choice with your focus. Are you strong enough to make the choice all other [5th graders] are making? Please show us."

THE COOPERATION
CHALLENGE

---

*"We may have all come on different ships,
but we're in the same boat now."*

— Martin Luther King, Jr.

CREATING A CLASSROOM ENSEMBLE THROUGH COOPERATION

"We all sink or we all swim."

If you have been on a team or worked in a group, you have probably heard that statement. While it sounds good and the sentiment behind it is, no doubt, well intended, things don't always work out that way. Sometimes some of us swim and let others sink. Sometimes some of us sink and drag others down with us. There is a fair share of people that have less than pleasant memories about group work in school. However, for cooperative learning to reach its maximum potential, and for drama to have the slightest chance at supporting the development of this skill, the concept of "we all sink or we all swim" must be made real and tangible. We do that by explicitly teaching and regularly implementing strategies that develop cooperation. As a collaborative art form, drama requires that all members of an acting ensemble do their part and help others do their part, too.

> *... for cooperative learning to reach its maximum potential... the concept of "we all sink or we all swim" must be made real and tangible.*

Cooperative learning is a form of social-emotional learning. Recent research findings show that social-emotional learning programs improve academic performance and general school performance. A meta-analysis involving more than 200 studies of social-emotional learning programs, found that students scored more than 10 points higher in academic achievement and had better school attendance, grades, and social interactions within the classroom [9].

Further research supports the efficacies of cooperative learning in particular [10]. How do we gracefully help students navigate the path to cooperative learning and success? The Cooperation Challenge, the next Acting Right strategy, will help students navigate that path. It requires teams to engage in quick decision-making and results in the creation of an ensemble, a group that works well together.

As with the fitness analogy I used earlier, cooperation is a muscle that only grows strong if it is exercised consistently. With the Cooperation Challenge, we exercise that muscle in three ways:

- In phase 1 we focus on inclusive grouping to create a strong sense of unity. This phase helps team members learn to welcome all its members and help them feel included. A feeling of "fairness" pervades this part of the activity.

- In phase 2 we focus on exclusive grouping to help team members learn to make decisions that will benefit the team, even if it means the decision may not appear to treat all members fairly or equally. This is the more challenging part of cooperation.

- Finally, phase 3 integrates both phase 1 and phase 2, where students are cooperating in a fluent, cohesive manner.

THE COOPERATION CHALLENGE: SCRIPT

"I use the Cooperation Challenge every time I need students to work together. Today, for example, for science, we're doing planet research projects and I needed them to work in groups of three on a Chrome Book (a mini laptop) for their research. All I did was lead them in a Cooperation Challenge to get them into groups of three. After doing the Cooperation Challenge a thousand times, they are completely comfortable working with anyone in the class. They see it as 'oooh, it's fun, we get to be social!' but I'm using it to get them in groups for learning science. Often when I'm teaching these strategies to other staff members, I say 'remember the days when grouping kids was a headache because this one couldn't work with that one, and this one got on that one's nerves?' Now, thanks to the Cooperation Challenge, I don't need to worry about that anymore. It has helped me build a cooperative classroom where my students work well with everyone."

– Carrie Chinners, fourth grade teacher

"The Cooperation Challenge is one of my favorite strategies. We deal with a lot of conflict at the school, and that's due to the enormous community issues that we deal with. When we start partnering students, we really start to see the impact of a lot of the issues that we're facing. There's a lot of bickering. A lot of learned ways of being very aggressive and conflict-oriented. The Cooperative Challenge exercises have really helped us to build their capacity to work with each other productively and to listen attentively."

– Winston Cox, principal

PHASE 1: INCLUSIVE GROUPING

The following exercise is a great workout for the cooperation "muscle." It challenges students to make a series of inclusive groups. Every challenge you give should result in every student being included in a group.

This activity begins with students standing in a large circle. Tell them to listen to your directions before moving. Your role is to maintain a quick pace and to observe, interpret, and respond to behaviors. *Once again, the words you will say are in italics.*

SCRIPT: 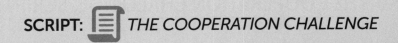 *THE COOPERATION CHALLENGE*

SETTING UP THE PLAYING FIELD

Let's see how strong your cooperation muscles are.

They are not here, [Point to arms]

and they are not here. [Point to legs]

They are here. [Point to head]

You will have to SHOW me your cooperation muscles are strong. Here's how you will show me.

*Right now, you are standing on the **Playing Field**.*

Your challenge on the Playing Field is to follow my directions.

*If you cannot follow my directions, you move from the Playing Field to a place in the game called the **Observation Deck**.*

We will talk more about that place later.

Let's talk more about the Playing Field.

When you are on the Playing Field, your challenge is to follow my directions. Here is an example of a direction I might give you. Don't do it, just listen.

I might say something like: "By the time I count to 3, you are in a group that has more than two people." Then I will count, one, two, three.

When I get to the number three, you must be in groups of more than two people or ALL OF US move to the Observation Deck.

Let me show you how to make a group. [Select three students]

If these three students made a group of more than two, I would know because they turn and face each other.

[Have the three students turn and face each other]

And, so I know they really agreed to make a group, they will put their hands on each other's shoulders. Not their backs, not their heads, but their shoulders. They also put their hands on the closest shoulder to them—not the farthest one—reaching around would turn it into a hug. This is not a hug, it is a group.

If one person's hand is not on their neighbor's shoulder, this is NOT a group and ALL OF US move to the Observation Deck.

I change the numbers each time. So, you have to be listening. And let's just say, in THIS game, ONE is not a group.

One more note: YOU WILL HAVE TO TALK in this game.

In a game like this, what do you think you will have to say?

[Students should respond: "Get in this group." "Put your hands on my shoulders."]

I will ONLY be giving you challenges where EVERYONE should be able to fit into a group. If someone is NOT in a group, it does not mean that student did not cooperate, it means the ENTIRE TEAM did not cooperate and we ALL move to the Observation Deck.

Setting Up the Observation Deck

Since you will be going to the Observation Deck at some point, let me show you where it is and what you do when you are there.

The Observation Deck is over here—in front of me—on the floor.

[Gesture to a place on the floor]

It is not beside me or behind me. It's not over there, or in that chair, or under that table. It is right here on the floor. When you are in the Observation Deck, you do three things. I will show you.

[Demonstrate]

1) The first thing you do is with your body—you sit down.

2) The second thing you do is with your voice—you turn it off.

3) The third thing you do is with your focal point—you make me your focal point.

You sit down, you are quiet, and you focus.

If you can sit down, control your voice, and stay focused, then you will be invited back to the Playing Field for the next round. If you are unable to sit down, control your voice, or focus while in the Observation Deck, you will not be invited back to the Playing Field for the next round.

The Observation Deck is NOT "Time Out." You are NOT in trouble. You are still in the game. It is just a place we will go to talk about what we did or observed on the Playing Field. The game of baseball has two places—we are either sitting in the dugout waiting to bat, or we are out playing on the field. In both places, we are still in the game.

Let me double-check my directions. By the time I count to 5—without running, pushing, or falling, EVERYONE is seated on the Observation Deck. Go! One, two, three, four, five. (Students move to the Observation Deck.)

I see everyone sitting down, quiet, and focused. How come no one is crying?

[Students should respond: "We are not in trouble."]

Just checking! Thanks for reminding me!

Now, the way you get from there BACK to the Playing Field is by controlling your body. You should be strong enough to choose to stand up and walk back. If you run, push, or fall down, we are ALL moving back to the Observation Deck to discuss what controlling our bodies means. Let's see who is strong enough to make the choice to control their body as they return to the Playing Field. Go! One, two, three, four, five

[Repeat if necessary]

Playing the Game

We are ready to play! Let's give it a try.

I am NOT playing; do not grab me.

Here we go:

[Give students challenges where they can all be in a group. Here are some suggestions:]

By the time I count to five, you are in a group that has more than three people.

One, two, three, four, five.

By the time I count to seven, you are in a group that has more than 5 people.

One, two, three, four, five, six, seven.

By the time I count to eight, you are in a group that has less than 5 people.

One, two, three, four, five, six, seven, eight.

By the time I count to four, you are in a group that has at least one boy.

One, two, three, four.

By the time I count to six, you are in a group that has at least one person with the letter M in their first name. One, two, three, four, five.

WHEN THEY FAIL

At any point in the activity, if every student is not in a group, send ALL the students to the Observation Deck and reflect on what happened. Reflection should lead them to understand that anything that happens to one of them, happens to all of them. It is everyone's job to look out for everyone else. We all sink, or we all swim.

Ask these questions in the Observation Deck:

*   *What happened?*

*   *Why didn't you do something about it?*

*   *What are you going to do differently when you come back?*

Challenge students to answer all questions beginning with the word "I." Beginning with an "I" statement will force students to take personal responsibility for what happened.

For example:

*   *What happened? "I noticed Marcus did not get into a group."*

*   *Why didn't you do something about it? "I was just happy that I got into a group and did not think about Marcus."*

*   *What are you going to do differently when you come back? "Once I take care of myself, I will look around and make sure everyone else is taken care of, as well."*

Once a few students have reflected and you feel the group has a plan in place, invite them to return to the Playing Field and try again. Repeat THE SAME challenge that caused them to go to the Observation Deck.

Play until the students have mastered the concept of including everyone, all the time. Once they do this, give them a challenge that gets them all into one big group, such as a group greater than 15. Once they are in one big group, continue to give them challenges where they should be able to stay as one big group, such as a group with at least one boy or a group where someone was born in the summer. If they stay as one group, you know they are thinking as one team. If they subdivide, they are not wrong, they have not yet developed group awareness. Keep playing until they do.

At this phase, everyone is on the Playing Field, or everyone is in the Observation Deck. We all move from one space to the next as a whole group.

HOW FAILURE LEADS TO SUCCESS

When students begin to play this game, you are in direct control of their success or failure. You can ensure their success if you slow your count or if you pause your counting until everyone has joined a group. Conversely, if you count quickly, without being responsive to what you see happening in front of you, the overly quick pace probably will ensure their failure.

The art of facilitating this game is to know when to create failure and when to create success. Too much success will make the game boring and will not reshape behaviors. Too much failure will result in burnout and make the students feel too defeated to continue trying. However, in the beginning, do not shy away from creating failure. Failure in the beginning will make the group try harder and focus faster.

When energy is too high – Because the Cooperation Challenge is a fast-paced game, the students' energy level can get very high, very quickly. If you need to temper the physical energy, simply count faster so that the students will fail at the exercise. Once they fail, you can move them to the Observation Deck, where you can reflect on the reason for the failure. Ensure that the students understand that the reason for their failure was their excess of energy.

It is not effective to tell students to calm down, because then they will associate high energy with a punitive discipline response. Instead, ask:

"When your energy is up here, what happens to your listening?" [Students should respond: You can't hear me.]

"To your eyes?" [Students should respond: You can't see what is happening.]

"To your brain?" [Students should respond: You can't think.]

Help the students construct the understanding that high energy makes them "black out" and makes them unsuccessful. If they want to be successful, they must lower their energy level.

The Cooperation Challenge teaches students to communicate with one another in a high-pressure environment while keeping their energy level under control. The end result, ideally, is the creation of an ensemble.

PHASE 2: EXCLUSIVE GROUPING

As we have just seen, inclusive grouping challenges students to make various groups where everyone can join a group. The Cooperation Challenge moves forward with exclusive grouping, which calls on students to make groups where everyone cannot join a group.

As you begin phase 2, remind students to listen to your directions before moving. Your role is still to maintain a quick pace and to observe, interpret, and respond to behaviors. Once again, the words you will say are in italics.

SCRIPT: 📄 *THE COOPERATION CHALLENGE*

We are ready for something more challenging now.

We have been playing so that everyone CAN join a group.

Now we are going to play so that everyone CANNOT get in a group.

When we played BEFORE, we knew we were winning if the entire team was on the Playing Field. We knew something had gone wrong if the entire team was in the Observation Deck.

When we play NOW, we will know we have won if, by the end, MOST of us are seated in the Observation Deck, and only two or three people are still on the Playing Field.

When we play this way, the number of people to be in a group will not work out. There will be some remainders. For the team to win, most of you, at some point, will need to make the choice to step BACK instead of stepping IN. If you step back, you will move to the Observation Deck. By the end, most of you will have needed to step back.

Does it matter if you step back and go to the Observation Deck? [Students should respond, "No."]

Does it matter if you stay on the Playing Field? [Students should respond, "No."]

What matters? [Students should respond, "That we work as a team."]

Let's see how you handle that. Here is a practice challenge:

[Use this if there is an odd number of students]

By the time I count to five, you are in a group that has ONLY two students. One, two, three, four, five.

[Use this if there is an even number of students]

By the time I count to five, you are in a group that has ONLY three students. One, two, three, four, five.

[In either case, at least one student will not be able to make it into a group. Reflect with the class this way:]

This student did not get in a group. When she could not get in a group, she had some choices. She could have:

- *Tried to trade places with someone else*
- *Tried to squeeze in the middle of a group*
- *Tried to hang on the outside of a group and pretend she was part of it*

Did she make any of those choices? [Students should respond, "No."]

If she had, what would have happened to this entire little group?

[Students should respond, "They would have all gone to the Observation Deck."]

So, would her choice have helped or hurt the team? [Students should respond, "Hurt."]

Would she have made a strong or a weak choice for cooperation? [Students should respond, "Weak."]

She did not make a weak choice. She chose simply to stand there.

Is she crying? Did she scream? Is she angry? [Students should respond, "No."]

She is calm, focused, and balanced.

By just standing there, did she help or hurt the team? [Students should respond, "Help."]

Did she make a strong or weak choice for cooperation? [Students should respond, "Strong."]

Will you be able to make the same strong choice as she did? We will see.

When you choose to step back, you will then move to the Observation Deck.

Now is when it is really FUN to be in the Observation Deck, because you get to watch the students on the Playing Field and observe what choices they make that keep them on the Playing Field or what choices they make that send them to the Observation Deck.

Just a reminder: The Observation Deck is a FUN place to be. You are NOT in trouble and it is NOT Time Out. You are still in the game.

Remember, the only way for our team to win now is for MOST of you to be in the Observation Deck by the end.

Let's give this new way a try!

As students begin to play the game, give them challenges that prevent them from being able to join a group. Here are some suggestions:

- *By the time I count to FIVE, you are in a group that only has THREE people. One, two, three, four, five. FREEZE!*

- *By the time I count to SEVEN, you are in a group that only has FIVE people. One, two, three, four, five, six, seven. FREEZE!*

- *By the time I count to EIGHT, you are in a group that only has ONE BOY and THREE GIRLS. One, two, three, four, five, six, seven, eight. FREEZE!*

- *By the time I count to FOUR, you are in a group that only has ONE BOY and ONE GIRL. One, two, three, four. FREEZE!*

As students begin to step back, thank them for their strong choice and send each of them to the Observation Deck. Continue to play until there are only two or three students remaining on the Playing Field. Play at this level until all have mastered exclusive groupings. You will know because the game will begin to be boring! Then proceed to phase 3.

Keep in mind:

- *Perspective is crucial in this game. You must shift the class's perspective on what behavior is perceived as "strong" and "weak." In this game, stepping out or away from a group because there are too many people is a very strong, cooperative choice. This must be highlighted. Keep in mind also that sometimes a group needs someone to step in. The student who does that is also making a "strong" choice. The strong or weak choice cannot be identified until the situation presents itself. That is what makes this game so challenging.*

- *The effectiveness of this game relies on the pace. Keep it quick. Each round should only take one to two minutes. If you do not think quickly on your feet, refer to the examples of ways to group students.*

- *Always play at least two rounds.*

- *At the end of a round, if someone is left on the Playing Field, it means the class's cooperation muscles are strong. The students give themselves a round of applause.*

- *Invite the students in the Observation Deck to count the number of groups and number of students within groups to problem solve how people could have formed different groups.*

PHASE 3: INCLUSIVE AND EXCLUSIVE GROUPING

Now play the game mixing directions that result in inclusive or exclusive groupings. If the students miss an inclusive grouping, send the entire class to the Observation Deck. If they step back because of an exclusive grouping, send only the students who stepped back to the Observation Deck.

Now you are ready to play again, but this time, you will not know if it is a challenge where everyone should be in a group or if some people will need to be strong enough to step back. I will keep mixing it up to see if you are really paying attention and cooperating!

ADVANCED CHALLENGES

Here are some advanced challenges to use when the class is ready or when they have no control of their voice and body.

Challenge #1: No Touching

This challenge is only for students who are in control of their bodies. If any student touches another student, they instantly move to the Observation Deck. Because they cannot touch, groupings are now made by keeping their arms by their sides and standing close to each other.

Challenge #2: No Talking

This challenge is only for students who are in control of their voices. If any student makes any sound with their voice, they instantly move to the Observation Deck.

Challenge #3: No Talking and Touching

This challenge is only for students who can control both their bodies and voices. If any student touches another student or makes a sound with their voice, they instantly move to the Observation Deck.

THE CLASS CHALLENGE

Establishing a learning environment where all students realize each person is an important and valuable member of the team is challenging. The Class Challenge is a great strategy to highlight for students that each one of them plays an important part on the team.

The following are examples of Class Challenges. If the entire class does not meet the challenge, the entire class returns to the Observation Deck.

- *Without talking, without touching, by the time I count to 10, the class has made one line.*

- *Without talking, without touching, by the time I count to 10, the class has made two lines (three lines, four lines, five lines, six lines).*
- *Without talking, without touching, by the time I count to 10, the class has made one circle.*
- *Without talking, without touching, by the time I count to four, one boy is in the middle of the circle (one girl, two girls, two boys, one boy and one girl, one boy who has not been in the middle, one girl who has not been in the middle, etc.).*

The highest level of the challenge is to work in silence without touching, however, Class Challenges can also be done where students can talk and touch.

ADVANCED Az GROUPINGS

BASICS	VOCABULARY	MATH
The same number of people as the number of days in a week	The same number of syllables as the word "Friday"	Even number
		Odd number more than one
The same number of people as the number of months in a year	The same number of letters as the word "Friday"	At least one boy
		Only one boy
	The same number of vowels as in the word "Friday"	At least one boy and one girl
		Only one boy and one girl
		More than two
		Greater than or equal to four
		Less than five
		No more than five
		The size of your group plus two
		Your group and two more
		The size of your group minus three
		The size of your group take away three
		The size of your group equals the sum of four plus three
		The size of your group has doubled
		The size of your group two times
		The size of your group has split in half
		The size of your group divided by two
		One, five times
		One times five

UNDERSTANDING THE OBSERVATION DECK

When students are playing the Cooperation Challenge, they typically understand that, conceptually, they are helping the team and are still winning if they step back from the group. However, some students are particularly competitive and will never make the choice to step out. Although they might give you all the right answers ("We are all winning even if we go to the Observation Deck!" "Yes, stepping back helps!"), they will not choose to step back because they still perceive that as losing. This is not group awareness.

As a solution, make it random. Thank the group for helping the team and ask them to go to the Observation Deck. The student who stepped out stays on the Playing Field. What you are doing is forcing students who won't step back to see that every choice they make on the Playing Field results in their perceived loss. They will see that the best way to play is to make the "right" choice, a choice not based on consequence.

Then you can ask the group, "What happens when you step back?" [We don't know.] "What happens if you step in?" [We don't know.] "Why would you make either choice?" [Because it helps the team.]

You are not forcing the understanding, but the actions to demonstrate the understanding. It is an intervention strategy. Use this method to reshape the perception of the Observation Deck and develop better understanding of exclusive grouping.

You can build comprehension further by engaging the Observation Deck. Once students are seated in the Observation Deck, it is much easier for them to see what is happening in the game and find alternate solutions. When they are taken off the Playing Field, the pressure is off. You can include them by asking questions and making commentary about what is happening on the Playing Field: Did you notice what they did? How many groups are left? How did the group solve that challenge?

Engage the students on the Observation Deck to help them understand that they are still in the game. They are winning, too. They just helped the game by stepping out.

REFLECTION QUESTIONS FOR STUDENTS

Taking time to reflect with students after engaging in the Cooperation Challenge is critical in helping them make sense of and learn from their experience. The following questions invite students to consider their feelings and thoughts about the Cooperation Challenge as well as transform their thinking.

Feel – *How does it feel to be on the Playing Field? The Observation Deck? How does it feel if someone makes faces or sounds or stomps their feet when moving to the Observation Deck? What does that say about their cooperation muscles?*

Think – *What are we learning by playing this game? Is it always "strong" to step in? To step out? What makes this game so challenging? What skills do we need to be successful in this game?*

Transform – *Why are these skills important in school? Home? Life? Who really "wins" in this game?*

COMMON PITFALLS IN FACILITATION

My experience providing instructional coaching to teachers leading the Cooperation Challenge has helped me uncover the following common pitfalls that are typically made when learning how to facilitate this strategy:

The pace is too slow – *One of the reasons these activities are so successful is due to their quick pace. The amount of time the students will tolerate being in the Observation Deck is limited. Each round should only be one to two minutes.*

Not prepared with grouping ideas – *It is acceptable to have a list of grouping ideas in your hand to help keep the pace quick. These activities should challenge the students to think on their feet, not you!*

Watching instead of counting – *You are the facilitator. As engaging as these activities are to watch, you must remember to count.*

FREQUENTLY ASKED QUESTIONS

In leading professional development workshops for teachers, the following questions typically arise regarding the use and facilitation of the Cooperation Challenge:

How often should I use the Cooperation Challenge?
I suggest using it every day at the beginning of the year and continuing for at least a month. Eventually, you will only need it for select moments throughout the year. However, continue to use the vocabulary of cooperation and making strong choices.

How long should we play?
Always play at least two rounds. Only playing one round is not enough for the students who move to the Observation Deck at the top of the round. About 10 minutes of this game is advised.

What do I do if a student stomps, sighs, cries, or pouts on the way to the Observation Deck?
Stop the game and ask the class how we move to the Observation Deck if we have strong cooperation muscles? What does it look like when we move to the Observation Deck with weak cooperation muscles? Then challenge them to always move to the Observation Deck demonstrating their strength.

How do I help the students realize that this is much more than a game?
After each round, while all the students are seated in the Observation Deck, reflect with them about the learning that is taking place. Ask them, "What are you learning by playing this game?" Without reflection, you are unsure what students are gaining from playing the game. Including reflection ensures that you can guide and shape the learning.

BENEFITS OF THE COOPERATION CHALLENGE

This exercise has multiple benefits in the classroom community, including:

- *Thinking Quickly*
- *Solving Problems*
- *Cooperating with Peers*
- *Listening to and Following Directions*
- *Developing Observation and Listening Skills*
- *Reinforcing Math Vocabulary and Skills*
- *Developing Multiple Intelligences: Intrapersonal, Interpersonal Intelligence, Bodily/Kinesthetic Intelligence, and Logical/Mathematical Intelligence*

ONE-MINUTE CHALLENGE
TABLEAU

"It is the long history of humankind (and animal kind, too) that those who learned to collaborate and improvise most effectively have prevailed."

— Charles Darwin

BECOMING FLUENT

When we teach reading comprehension, we teach students a number of proven strategies including looking for context clues, making connections, visualizing, and questioning. When students become fluent readers, they integrate the various strategies. Their use of the strategies becomes quite seamless and somewhat instinctive. They have developed reading fluency.

The same is true for the Acting Right strategies. As students progress across strategies—from the Actor's Toolbox, to the Concentration Circle, to the Cooperation Challenge—they build skills, competencies, and confidence, through practice over time.

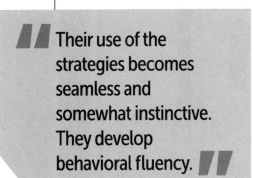

Their use of the strategies becomes seamless and somewhat instinctive. They develop behavioral fluency.

This final Acting Right strategy, the One-Minute Challenge Tableau, puts students' behavioral fluency to the test. It requires students to put in action all the behaviors they have learned through the prior Acting Right strategies. The activity forces them to demonstrate the strength of their cooperation, collaboration, and concentration "muscles." Students will be aware that effective group work requires many skills, such as leadership, collaboration, compromise, and problem-solving.

THE PHYSICAL LEARNER

The One-Minute Challenge Tableau uses a theatrical strategy to engage students in creating "living pictures" that capture a moment in time. More than any other Acting Right activity, this exercise is very physical and, as such, is highly appealing and motivating. Research in neuroscience points to evidence that the combination of mental and physical activities embodied in the arts is essential to brain development[11].

David Sousa, author of *How the Brain Learns*, suggests that even moderate physical activity increases oxygen in the blood, which enhances brain function and cognitive performance. What's more, Sousa says, movement consumes kinesthetic energy so that students can settle down and concentrate. What young children understand as play—singing, dancing, drawing—are art forms that engage the senses and prepare the brain for successful learning[12].

ONE-MINUTE CHALLENGE TABLEAU: SCRIPT

"In traditional teaching, we may ask students to raise their hand to provide an answer, or we may give them a worksheet to answer a question or two. When we do that, we're eliminating the power of social learning. When we use the One-Minute Challenge Tableau, we are using all the knowledge and understandings that each child in the group brings to the situation. They're learning from one another, which is really powerful."

"One-Minute Challenge Tableaus are quick and everyone's engaged, so it's a valuable teaching tool that saves teachers time rather than adds to the length of the lesson. If you ask students to raise their hands to tell you what they know, you may hear from three or four students in a three- or four-minute period, whereas when they do a One-Minute Challenge Tableau, every child is engaged, more voices are heard, and in less than three or four minutes, you have checked in with all of them. More voices are heard when they're engaging in One Minute Challenge Tableaus—which is important."

– Melanie Rick, national Acting Right consultant

"The One-Minute Challenge Tableau is our strongest Common Core approach because it exercises every child's speaking and listening skills. They need to construct understanding together, which means they need to build upon each other's ideas. It scaffolds how they build in their ideas so that it ensures every child is speaking. It provides teachers an opportunity to listen in to each child's thinking."

– Rae Takemoto, arts integration curriculum coordinator

The following exercise challenges students to work in teams to create visual models of their thinking—a living picture—a tableau. To begin, create small groups with three to five students per group. Mixed-gender groupings tend to work best. Have the small groups sit in a circle facing each other.

Ask students to make you their focal point and then begin the script below. *Again, the words you will say are in italics.*

SCRIPT: 📄 THE ONE-MINUTE CHALLENGE TABLEAU

Your group is about to create a picture together.

Not a picture like a camera takes, but a living picture—one you will make with your bodies.

When actors make a picture, they don't call it a picture. They call it a tableau. Tableau is French for picture. I will teach you a four-step process for creating a tableau.

Let's start at the beginning.

STEP 1: Think

I will give you the challenge for what your group will make.

*So, the first thing you will do is **THINK** silently. When you have an idea, you will not talk. You will not whisper. You will not make faces. You will simply pull that idea in close, by crossing your arms. Just like this.* [**Cross arms**]

Let's give it a try.

For our first tableau, you will create a tableau that shows something that has wings.

Silently THINK to yourself, "What do I know that has wings?" When you have an idea, pull it in close and cross your arms. We are not talking.

[**Watch and wait for all students to cross arms**]

STEP 2: Share

*The next step is to **SHARE** your ideas with your small group.*

Everyone will have a chance to share their idea quickly. This is how you will do it.

Let's imagine I am in this group. [**Point to a group**]

I start by opening my arms and letting my idea go.
[**Show opening arms**]

I say, "I was thinking...a butterfly."

After I say that, I am quiet. I put my hands on my legs and I am done. Everyone in my group listened to my idea, but no one says anything about it.

[Point to someone in group] *She does not say, "I love butterflies" or "We had pet butterflies in kindergarten" or "That was MY idea" or "Yeah, let's make that!"*

I say, "I was thinking...butterflies." And then no one says anything.

The next person uncrosses their arms and says their idea. Everyone listens. She may say, "I was thinking...bats." And then she is quiet and puts her hands on her legs. No one says anything about her idea.

[Point to someone in group] *She does not say, "I hate bats" or "We have a bat in our attic" or "I was a bat for Halloween" or "Yeah, let's make a bat."*

So far, this is what it sounds like: "I was thinking...butterflies." "I was thinking...bats."

Then the next person shares, and then the next. After about 10 seconds, all arms are uncrossed, hands are on legs and no one is talking.

Let's try it.

One person start by saying, "I was thinking." Go.

[Watch and listen as groups share. If you hear students adding thoughts, extending the conversation, or choosing what to make, stop them and have them start again.]

STEP 3: Plan

*When everyone has shared, it will be time for your group to select an idea and come up with a **PLAN** for making the tableau.*

When you plan, you will start by asking this question:

"What should we make?"

Your group will have only 10 seconds to answer that question. After 10 seconds, everyone in your group should know the answer. Everyone in your group should have the SAME answer.

I will give you a test. After 10 seconds, I will point to anyone and say, "What should we make?" Whomever I point to has to say the answer JUST LIKE THAT. [Snap fingers]

She can't say, "Well...um...ah..." Those sounds make me think she is just making it up right then.

If I say, "What should we make?" to her, HE cannot answer for her. [Point to someone in group]

If I say, "What should we make?" to her and she answers, and then I look at him and say, "What should we make?" he has to have the SAME answer.

If you have ANY time left over, go around the circle and have each person practice saying the answer.

Don't start deciding HOW you will make this or WHAT parts you will play. Just answer the question "What should we make?"

Give it try.

Ready, go!

[Watch and listen as groups plan. If you hear students going beyond the question "What should we make?" then stop them and have them start again.]

[After about 10 seconds, stop them and randomly ask a few "What should we make?" Be a tough judge. Don't accept any hesitation, ums or ahs. This is a typical red flag for uncertainty. You want the groups to empower each other with confidence by practicing the answer. Call on at least two people in each group and make sure they have the same answer. If they don't have it or hesitate in answering, give every group 10 more seconds to rehearse again and tighten it up. Then test them again and again, until they have it.]

Now that you know WHAT your group will make, let's move on to the second question we ask when we PLAN:

"What parts will we need?"

Whatever you have decided to make, has some parts. If my group decided to make a butterfly, we would need these parts [counting on fingers]:

We need a body.

We need wings.

We need a head.

We need antennae.

We need four parts. There are four people in our group, so four parts makes sense. We can't have 10 parts if there are only four people. We many have three parts, or even five, but too many won't work for four people. Notice how I used my fingers to count the parts. Also notice that I kept saying, "We need...," "We need...," "We need... ."

When you answer this question "What parts do we need?" you should use your fingers to count the parts and I should hear you saying "We need...," "We need...," "We need... ."

If you have any time left, go around the circle and make sure everyone can name the parts you need.

I will give you another test in 10 seconds. Go!

[Watch and listen as groups plan. If you hear students going beyond the question "What parts do we need?" then stop them and have them start again.]

[After about 10 seconds, stop them and randomly ask a few students, "What parts do we need?" Be a tough judge. Don't accept any ums or ahs. If they don't have it, give every group 10 more seconds to tighten it up, and then test again and again until they have it.]

To complete our PLAN, the last question we are answering:

"What part will you play?"

Take 10 seconds and make sure everyone in your group knows which part they are playing. They should be able to say, "I will play the...wings" or "I will play the body..." Go!

[Give groups about 10 seconds to figure this out. Make sure they stay seated and do not begin to make it with their bodies.]

STEP 4: CREATE

You know what you are making. You know what parts you need, and you know what part you will play. We are ready for the fourth and last step, CREATE.

When I say "go," your group will have 30 seconds to make your PLAN happen—to make the picture with your bodies.

At the end of 30 seconds, everyone in your group will be frozen in place, their bodies will look like the part they just agreed to play, and their eyes will be locked on a focal point. Nothing will be moving. Not even your hair.

Everyone cannot lay down to make this. Everyone cannot stand up to make this. You will need people at different physical levels. [Use your hands to show low, medium, and high levels.] And we can't use furniture or props to help us out.

You have 30 seconds to CREATE. Go!

[Give groups about 30 seconds to create. They are usually finished in under 30 seconds. Don't wait until it looks like everyone is ready. That will take too long. After about 30 seconds say:]

You have 10 seconds left. [Count slowly as they finalize their tableau] *Ten, nine, eight, seven, six, five, four, three, two, one. Lock your eyes on a focal point. Show you are in control of body and voice. If you are laughing, moving, or talking, you have LOST control and will take your entire group to the Observation Deck.*

[As you look around at the groups, make sure everyone is frozen and focused and looks as if they are playing a part. If not, give them 10 more seconds to fix it. Once groups are ready, do not critique—just make observations or use questioning. Say things like:]

"Interesting."

"I see it."

"Yes."

"What is it I'm looking at?"

"Do I see it?"

[Then say:]

...and relax your bodies! Unfreeze. Have a seat back in a circle with your small group.

The procedural script for the One-Minute Challenge Tableau is quite lengthy, but the actual creative process is not. Here is a review of the steps:

1. *Think*

2. *Share*

3. *Plan*
   - *What should we make?*
   - *What parts do we need?*
   - *What part will you play?*

4. *Create*

SCRIPT: *GRADUAL RELEASE OF RESPONSIBILITY*

This procedure may take 10 to 15 minutes to explain the first time. You will probably have to guide students through this process, step by step, several times until you feel confident they understand what is required at each step and they are able to execute each step with fidelity. Once this is in place, you can begin to speed up the process a bit. The next, quicker phase would sound like this:

The next tableau you are going to create in your small group will be a tableau that shows something that requires electricity. We are at Step 1: Think. So, cross your arms when you have an idea of something that requires electricity.

[When everyone has their arms crossed, continue]

"When I say go, you will have 30 seconds to:

Share and plan. Ready? Go!"

[After about 30 seconds, call time and say:]

Raise your hand if your group DOES NOT have a plan.

[If someone raises their hand, say:]

Everyone has 10 more seconds to get it or to review the plan they have! Go!

[Check in again. When no one raises their hand say:]

Your group now has 30 seconds to create. Go!

[Finally, you are ready to stop checking in and regulating this creative process. It is time for the process to become fluent. Here is what you would say:]

The next tableau your group is going to create is going to show me something that you would see at a circus. We are at Step 1: Think. Cross your arms when you have an idea of something you would see at a circus.

[When everyone has their arms crossed, continue]

When I say go, you will have one minute to:

Share, plan and create. I won't be stopping you along the way. Ready? Go!

[When you see groups beginning to stand up to create their tableaus, call out "10 more seconds." You should notice groups beginning to scramble to get in place once you make this call. After about five more seconds, begin to count down from 10, as all groups move into place.]

IDEAS FOR ONE-MINUTE CHALLENGE TABLEAU

Depending on your students' age and level of experience, you can choose tableau challenges that are concrete or abstract, simple or complex. Some options are provided below:

CONCRETE
- *Letters*
- *Shapes*
- *Objects - Nouns*

MODERATELY ADVANCED
- *Things that start with the letter __*
- *Things that have _____ [number] of syllables*
- *Things that have a long ___ [letter] sound*
- *Things that grow*
- *Things that swim*
- *Things we find in a forest*
- *Vocabulary words*

ABSTRACT
- *Themes/Concepts*
- *People*
- *Historical periods*
- *Colors*

ADVANCED
- *Recreate paintings (from art cards)*
- *Recreate illustrations from picture books*
- *Recreate book covers*
- *Create a picture of a chapter from a book*
- *Create a cover for a book*
- *Create a poster image for a historical period or science topic*

REFLECTION QUESTIONS FOR STUDENTS

Taking time to reflect with students after engaging in One-Minute Challenge Tableau is critical in helping them make sense of and learn from their experience. The following questions invite students to consider their feelings and thoughts about One-Minute Challenge Tableau as well as transform their thinking.

Feel

How does it feel to work together as a team?

What did it feel like to have a limited amount of time to create together?

Think

What is challenging about the One-Minute Challenge Tableau?

How is showing what you know through tableau different from showing what you know through writing?

How did your group agree on what to make?

Were you able to use everyone's ideas? Why or why not?

Transform

How did the One-Minute Challenge Tableau help you better understand [x]?

COMMON PITFALLS IN FACILITATION

My experience providing instructional coaching to teachers leading One-Minute Challenge Tableaus has helped me uncover the following common pitfalls that are typically made when learning how to facilitate this strategy:

Timing is too fast or too slow – Although this activity is called "One-Minute Challenge Tableau," each challenge rarely takes a minute. Many times, the challenge unfolds faster, and occasionally it unfolds slower than one minute. What is important is that you use your observations to guide the amount of time you give the groups. If you give too much time, groups will typically go off task and begin to misbehave. If you give too little time, groups will get frustrated with each other and the process. The art of facilitating these challenges is gauging how much time to give each one. As a guide, most challenges rarely take more than 30 seconds.

Limiting the amount of time for groups to work provides positive pressure. When groups decide what to create, you can jump in with a 10-second warning. The short time frame is given so that students' will think there is a limited amount of time and reduce the time they use to argue or go off task. However, as a general rule, do not tell students you are giving them less or more time.

The teacher is helping the students – As hard as it will be, stay out of the group work! This activity is created for the group to solve. If there is no leader in the group, be patient; one will emerge. If there are too many leaders, be patient; some will become team members. Assisting the groups builds their dependence on adult help and robs them of the chance to problem-solve as a group. Avoid reinforcing learned helplessness.

There is too much emphasis on product – The objective of this strategy is cooperation and collaboration, not product. Avoid placing a judgment on what the group creates. Do not walk around and say, "Oh, that is great" or "Look at theirs!" or "That does not look like a [X]." If students are frozen and no one is upset, that is a good signal that they have worked together as a team!

FREQUENTLY ASKED QUESTIONS

In leading professional development workshops for teachers the following questions typically arise regarding the use and facilitation of One-Minute Challenge Tableau:

How often should I use this activity?
I would use the One-Minute Challenge Tableau every day until students are able to navigate the four-step process on their own, in about a minute.

How many One-Minute Challenge Tableaus should I do each time?
It is helpful to do each challenge at least two or three times. This allows the small groups to figure out their dynamics and adjust accordingly.

What do I do if a small group is unable to complete the challenge?
A group that fails to complete the challenge does so for one of three reasons:

- *First, they did not hear the challenge. The group was talking when you gave the challenge. Do not repeat the challenge. Let the group feel the weight of failure. At the end of the challenge, make sure they understand that their failure was due to their lack of voice control and concentration. Remind them that listening is their responsibility and you will not speak louder or repeat the challenges.*

- *Second, they just did not understand the challenge or do not know how to physically demonstrate it. In this case, I use the other groups who were capable of completing the challenge to be the models. The group that was unable to complete the challenge goes on a "gallery walk" to see how the other groups have solved the problem.*

- *Third, the group was unable or unwilling to cooperate. In this instance, I ask the entire group to sit in the Observation Deck (see Cooperation Challenge) and observe the next challenge. I sit with the group and help them observe and reflect on what the other groups are doing to cooperate, such as taking turns, sharing ideas, being strong enough to take ideas out or put them in. At the end of the challenge, I ask the group what they learned by observing. Those who respond are invited back for the next challenge.*

You said the emphasis should not be on product, but I think One-Minute Challenge Tableaus can be used to assess students' understanding in content areas as well as to teach cooperation. Is this wrong?
When your students are skilled at navigating the process of creating tableaus, you may be interested in learning how to use the tableau strategy as an instructional tool. Tableaus can be used extremely effectively across the curriculum as not just a means of engaging students but also for differentiating instruction and assessing student comprehension. I

have developed an entire body of work to help teachers learn this strategy. Stay tuned for my next book.

BENEFITS OF ONE-MINUTE CHALLENGE TABLEAU

Now that you have become familiar with the One-Minute Challenge Tableau, its benefits for the classroom community are evident:

- *Builds Teams*
- *Develops Skills in Collaboration*
- *Supports Problem Solving*
- *Supports Multiple Intelligences, including Visual/Spatial, Interpersonal, and Bodily Kinesthetic*
- *Builds Leadership Skills*
- *Opportunities for Brainstorming*

EARLY CHILDHOOD ADAPTATIONS

"If children grew up according to early indications, we should have nothing but geniuses."

— Johann Wolfgang von Goethe

MAKING IT WORK FOR THE LITTLE ONES

As established earlier, behavior is a literacy, like reading. With reading, our work with young children focuses on pre-emergent reading skills, building blocks, foundational entry points. And it is the same with the Acting Right strategies.

According to the National Association for the Education of Young Children, effective and developmentally-appropriate teaching strategies for early childhood include:

- Acknowledging what children do or say.
- Encouraging persistence and effort rather than just praising what a child has done.
- Giving specific feedback rather than general comments.
- Modeling attitudes, ways of approaching problems, and behavior toward others.
- Asking questions that provoke children's thinking.
- Giving directions for children's behavior.
- Creating challenge so that a task goes beyond what the children can already do.

From the approaches we use to the vocabulary we use, each of these tactics has a solid place in the Acting Right strategies (which are designed for K-12 students). For the Acting Right strategies to be most effective with young children, many times, developmentally appropriate adaptations should be made. Young children benefit from the activities that are broken down into smaller steps and taken at a slower pace. Some exercises may require a deeper explanation as the children do not have the same foundational knowledge that older students have. We must also keep in mind that young children may not be ready to work in groups or stand for long periods of time.

With these variations and the ones that follow, the Acting Right strategies are just as effective as they are with older students. (Note that the early childhood adaptations can double as modifications for students of any age with special needs.)

THE ACTOR'S TOOLBOX

To help young children gain a deeper understanding of the five tools of the Actor's Toolbox, take one or two days to use the following procedures as an introduction. Again, the words you will say are in italics. For these procedures, have students sit with you in a large circle on the floor.

THE NEED FOR TOOLS

1. Show the students pictures of three to four occupations (e.g., chef, banker, doctor, painter). Point out that each of these people has certain tools that they bring to work each day. For example, what "tools" would a fireman need? A banker? A teacher? Point out that if these people don't have their tools, they won't be able to do their jobs well.

2. Explain to students that they, too, have a job—to be a student. As students, they need to bring five tools to school with them each day. Ask students to count to five, using the fingers on one hand, to help them remember there are five tools.

YOU SAY:

We're going to call our five tools the Actor's Toolbox because, in addition to being students, we are also going to be actors. Actors are people who pretend to be someone or something else. As actors, we're going to need an actor's workout. Actors don't work out these muscles. (Point to arms) Actors don't work out these muscles. (Point to legs) Actors work out these muscles. (Point to your brain) Let's start our workout with tool #1, the first tool!

TOOL 1 THE BODY

PREPARATION: *Make five Tool Cards using the templates found at the end of this chapter. Put the five Tool Cards in a bag.*

1. Begin the activity by removing the Tool Card for body.
    What is the word on this card? Can you figure it out based on the picture? **(Students respond)** *The first tool is our body. Each day we bring our bodies to school, and we need to be able to control our bodies.*

2. *Let's see how well you can control your body by playing a short game of Simon Says.* **(Give several commands using the stem "Simon says tell your body to..." For example, Simon says tell your body to stand up. Simon says, tell your body to jump up and down. Simon says tell your body to wave to your teacher. Simon says tell your body to wiggle. Simon says sit down.)**

3. *You just did several things with your body—stand, wiggle, jump. I gave you the directions but I didn't control your body. WHO controls your body?* **(Lead children to understand that they do.)**

Can [Lee] make [Jennifer's] body jump? No, only [Jennifer] can make her body jump.

3. *YOU are the person who controls your body. That's good to know because during the day, you'll need to tell your body to do different things. For example, I may ask you to stand on the carpet.* **(Model what a strong choice and weak choice would look like. Be sure to use the words "strong" and "weak." Let them show you "strong" and "weak" based on that direction.)** *Other times, I may ask to you sit on the rug. (Model strong and weak choices. Have them join you.)*

4. Describe a few other things your body may be doing, for example throwing a ball, walking in line, moving like a snake. Lead students to understand that controlling your body doesn't mean being still all the time. It means being able to tell your body what to do to match the teacher's directions.

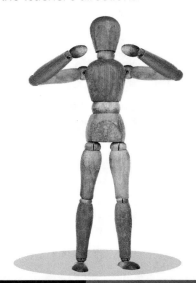

TOOL 2   THE VOICE

1. Remove the second Tool Card from the bag.
    The second tool in our toolbox is our voice.

2. *Let's use our voice to say the beginning of a song you may know. If you think you know the song, join in with me.* **(Begin singing the song)** *The wheels on the bus go round and round, round and round, round and round. The wheels on the bus go round and round, all through the town.*

3. *Now, we'll going to play a game called the "Volume Control Game." We'll sing the same song and we'll try different ways to control our voice.*
    (Use a CD player to show what the volume button does. Pretend to pull something—the Volume Control button—out of your pocket. Put your hands together so that it looks like you are holding it carefully.)
    When I hold the volume control at my waist, it means we are using a medium, inside voice. When I hold the volume control up in the air, I am using a loud, shouting voice. When I hold the volume control button down to my knees, I am using a quiet, whisper voice. **(Model all three)**

4. Explain to students that they are going to sing the song again, but this time the class has to watch the volume control button to know HOW to control their voice. Go through the song, moving the imaginary control button/your hand up and down. Then, allow a child to "hold" the volume control button. Hand the imaginary button carefully to the child and tell the child to hold it tightly. If time allows, invite another child to move the button. Then, take back the imaginary button and pretend to put it in a special place for use at a later time.

5. Explain how you could also change your voice by sounding like different characters such as papa voice, squeaky mouse voice. You may want to repeat the song using one of those voices.

6. Point out that we just learned how we control our body, which means we tell our body what to do. Who controls our voice? *(Lead students to understand that they control their voices.)*

7. *Since YOU tell your voice what to do, YOU are the person who controls your voice. That's good to know because during the day, you'll need to tell your voice to do different things. For example, I may ask you to tell your neighbor what you ate for breakfast this morning. If everyone is talking to their neighbor at once, it may get too loud. We might need to control the volume of our voices. What would a strong choice sound like? What would a weak choice sound like?* **(Give other examples that are pertinent to your class. Make sure students understand that voice control does not mean always being quiet.)**

TOOL 3 THE IMAGINATION

1. *Now we're ready for the third tool.*
    (Remove the card labeled "Imagination." Ask students to say the word with you.)
    Does anyone know what imagination means?
    (Lead students to understand that it's a part of our brain that helps us pretend.)

2. *I'm going to show you one way I can use my imagination.*
   (Pull out a piece of paper. Roll it up into a cylindrical shape. Then, pretend like you are brushing your teeth with the piece of paper. See if students can figure out that you are pretending the paper is a toothbrush).
   Did the paper really become a toothbrush? No. I used my imagination to pretend it did.
   (Give another example. Fold the paper flat and begin "combing" your hair. See if students can figure out how the paper has changed into a comb.)
   Did the paper really become a comb? No. I used my imagination.

3. *Now let's see how well you can use your imagination. When, I count to three, I want to see if you can make a statue of something. A statue is frozen. It doesn't move at all. Let me show you. I am going to make a statue of a dinosaur.* **(Model a statue of a dinosaur)**

4. *By the time I count to three, use your imagination to make a statue of a dinosaur. One-two-three FREEZE!*
   (Check to make sure everyone is frozen)
   Now, when I say, "Go," your statue will come to life. You'll be moving around like a dinosaur until you hear this sound **(Tap a small drum, tambourine, etc.)**.
   (Give students a few examples: becoming a frog, elephant, painter to create as statues, come to life, and then freeze at the sound.)

5. *Let's use our imagination another way.*
   (Place your hands at the temples of your head)
   I'm going to close my eyes and use my imagination to go anywhere in the universe I want to go. Someplace that will make me happy. I am going to go to the beach. I will be right back!
   (Pause a few seconds with your eyes closed. Then, open your eyes.)
   I'm back in our class now. Now close YOUR eyes and let your imagination take you anywhere you want to be that would make YOU happy. It might be at grandma's house, on a boat, or at the ice cream shop!
   (Pause until everyone has closed their eyes)
   Now, open your eyes. You're back in the classroom. If you'd like to share where your imagination took you, put your hands on your knees.
   (Invite a few to share)

TOOL 4 CONCENTRATION

1. Remove the next Tool Card—concentration.
    Our next tool is concentration. We have to really build our concentration muscles. They're not here. **(Point to arms)** *They're not here.* **(Point to legs)** *They're here.* **(Point to brain)**

2. Put an object, like a stuffed animal—for example Curious George—on a stool in the center of the circle of students. Tell students you're going to lock your eyes on Curious George. Lock your eyes on Curious George. Keep your eyes locked while you continue to explain.
    I'm going to lock my eyes on Curious George. I'm going to call him my focal point because he is the one point that is getting all my focus and attention. If my concentration muscles are STRONG, I'll keep my eyes locked on Curious George without looking around, laughing, smiling, or talking. If my concentration muscles are SUPER STRONG, I can do this for at least 10 seconds. Now I'm going to take my eyes off my focal point.
    (Return to a normal gaze and look at students)

3. *I want you to watch me to see if I'm holding onto my concentration. Look at my eyes to see if they stay locked on the focal point—Curious George—as I count to 10. One, two, three, four, five, six, seven, eight, nine, ten.. Now I'm going to take my eyes off my focal point. Were my concentration muscles strong? How could you tell? What did you see me doing?*

4. *Now I'm going to show you what would happen if my muscles were weak.* **(Start counting one, two, three, etc. Look around, move your body, etc.)** *What did you see me do that time?* **(Students respond)** *When my brain wanted me to peek around, I gave in. I should have told my brain, "No. Look at Curious George. Look at Curious George." I have to tell my brain what to do. I need to be the boss of my brain—not let my brain be the boss of me!*

5. *Now let's see if your concentration muscles are strong. Let's see if YOU can be the boss of your brain. Let's see if you can keep your eyes locked on Curious George for five seconds. Lock your eyes. Go. One, two, three, four, five.*
(If you see children looking away, point at Curious George and say, "Eyes on Curious George." You may need to remind students to blink.)

6. *Our focal point often changes throughout the day. Let me find something else in the room that would be interesting.*
(Find an object. Make that the new focal point. Ask students to look at that new focal point for five counts.)

7. Next, ask students to find something in the room that they find interesting. Ask them to point to it. Pick one student's object of interest. That will be the new focal point. The goal here is for students to begin to understand that building concentration means our eyes stay locked on a focal point.

8. Challenge students to focus on something for longer periods of time; while you count to higher and higher numbers.

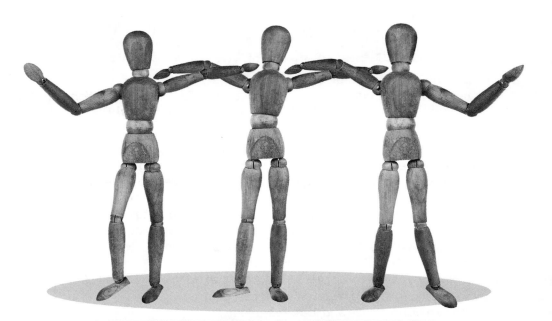

TOOL 5 COOPERATION

1. Remove the last card—cooperation.
The last tool is cooperation. That's another long word that begins with the letter "C". We just learned about concentration.
(Ask students say that word with you.)
That's when we tell our brain where to lock our eyes. Now we're going to find out about cooperation.

2. *Look at the picture on the card. What does it look like the figures are doing?* **(Lead students to understand that cooperation has to do with working together.)** *This year, we'll be cooperating with each other. That means we'll help each other, share with each other, and be kind to others. For example, if* **(name)** *dropped something on the ground, I might cooperate with him by picking it up. What if* **(name)** *had her hands full and needed to open the door? How could I cooperate with that person?* **(Give a couple of other examples of how to cooperate at different places in the room, e.g., centers, lunchroom, etc.)**

3. *Let's play a game to see how strong our cooperation muscles are.* **(Ask the student all sit on the floor in front of you, not behind or beside you.)** *Let's say that you are all now sitting in a place called the Observation Deck. Because when you are sitting here, you will observe—look—watch. I want you to sit here in the Observation Deck and watch how we get into groups. You will only watch for a little bit. Then you will all be playing. Let's start with two people.* **(Invite two students, who you think will be strong models for this work, to stand in front of the group. Choose a boy and a girl.)**

4. *Let's watch* **(girl's name)** *and* **(boy's name)**. *If I said, "Get into a group that has TWO people," this is how they would do it.* **(Girl name)** *and* **(boy name)** *would stand in front of each other and put their hands on each other's shoulders.* **(Demonstrate with the two students.)** *That is what a group looks like. They are not squeezing, dancing, laughing, or talking.* **(Ask the students to lower their arms)** *Let's look again. Get into a group that has two people.* **(Boy and girl make group)** *Let's make this more challenging!*

5. **(Invite another boy and girl to join you. There will be four students standing.)** *Watch this: Get into a group that has two people.* **(Students form two groups)** *Let's make this MORE challenging. Make a group that has FOUR people.* **(See if students can form one circle of four. If not, assist them.)** *This is what a group of FOUR looks like. Now show me a group of two. Now show me a group of four.* **(Students do each grouping while the others watch)**

6. Continue to call up two students at a time, adding to the standing group. Each time, start with directions to make groups of TWO. Then mix it up with directions to make groups of THREE or FOUR or groups with two girls and two boys.

7. Eventually you will have the entire class standing and participating. Keep those students seated who you feel would benefit the most from observing the longest.

8. As you facilitate this grouping activity, monitor how the students play. If someone grabs or runs or is being silly, simply stop and say, *"That is not how we said we would play THIS game."*

In early childhood, simply having students become aware of their bodies in space and that there are others around them is a big step. This modified set-up also allows for students to slowly develop their external focus as well as self-regulate their energy when working with a large group.

ALL 5 TOOLS

When all five tools in the Actor's Toolbox have been modeled, discussed, and experienced, you are ready to put them together.

1. *Now, let's see if we can put all five tools together.*
   (Begin by naming the five tools while you model the movements of the contract. Model twice and then, invite the students to join you.)

2. After leading the work for a day or two, explain how the movements are a contract, agreement, or promise. Follow the Actor's Toolbox script to teach students to sign the contract silently and in a calm, focused, and balanced state.

ONE-MINUTE CHALLENGE TABLEAU

INTRODUCTION

1. Place students in the Observation Deck.

2. Have two of the strongest-thinking students come to the Playing Field sitting "knee-to-knee" and "eye-to-eye."

3. *I'm getting ready to give these two students a challenge. The challenge involves creating a picture of an ice cream cone. But if you notice, I didn't hand them any crayons, paper, or paint. That is because they're going to be making the picture using their bodies. They're going to work together to create one frozen picture, or a tableau, of an ice cream cone. A tableau is a frozen picture we make with our bodies.*

4. *In order to create a tableau, these students are going to follow four steps. We'll go through each of the steps so that you can see what they look like.*

   - **THINK** – *The first step is to think. If I was going to think about an ice cream cone, this is what thinking looks like.* **(Model having a serious expression concentrating on something)**

     This is what thinking sounds like. **(Continue modeling "thinking" without saying anything)**

     Could you tell what I was thinking? No? Why? Because on the outside, thinking is quiet. It may appear that I'm not doing anything at all. But on the inside, my mind is busy. On the inside, I'm saying to myself, "When I think about an ice cream cone, I see one of those waffle cones with chocolate and strawberry ice cream on top." When I have thought of an idea, I pull it in closely and hold onto it like this **(cross arms)**.

     I'm going to give these two students about 10 seconds to think about what their ice cream cone would look like. Does their ice cream cone have to look like mine? No! I hope they think of different types of ice cream cones.

*(**Look at the two students**) When you have thought of your ice cream cone, cross your arms. That lets me know you've got your picture of an ice cream cone in your mind.*
(Give the two students a few seconds to think. Check to see if they have crossed their arms.)

- **SHARE** – *The second step is to share. Now that they have thought about ice cream cones, it is time for them to share their ideas with each other. This is how they will share. One of them starts by letting their idea go, by opening their arms and letting the idea go like this **(show opening arms)**.*

  *And they say, "I was thinking..." and they share what they were thinking about ice cream cones. Let's listen to these two SHARE. One starts by saying, "This is what I was thinking." Let's listen. **(Facilitate the two students sharing.)***

- **PLAN** – *The third step is to PLAN. When they have shared their ideas, it's time to for them come up with a PLAN for making the ice cream cone. They start by asking this question: "What should we make?" Let's listen.*

  (Both students ask that question)

  *We already know WHAT we are making. What is the answer? **(Ice cream cone)***

  *Next we ask this question: "What PARTS will we need?" What parts will we need if we are making an ice cream cone? **(Students respond)***

  *Right! We need a cone and we need ice cream. Two parts. There are two people. So, the last PLANNING question is "What PART will you play?" One person looks at the other and asks that question, "What part will you play?" She might say, "I will play the ice cream." If she says that, he does not say, "I wanted to play the ice cream!" If she says, "I will play the ice cream," he says, "Ok, I will play the cone." But what if he DID say, "Hey, I want to play the ice cream!" What would she say? She would say, "Okay, then I will play the cone." Let's listen as one asks and answers the question, "What part will you play?" **(Facilitate the two students selecting parts)***

- **CREATE** – *They know what they are making—an ice cream cone. They know what parts they need—ice cream and a cone. They know what part they will play—he will play the ice cream, and she will play the cone. We are ready for the fourth and last step, CREATE. They will need to make the ice cream cone with their bodies. If she is goSing to be the cone, what will her body shape look like? Will she be tall or short? She will be a tall cone shape? Let's see how she makes that with her body. **(Facilitate student making cone shape with body)***

  *If he is the ice cream, what will his body shape look like? Round or square? Where on the cone would he be? On top. Right! But can he put his whole body up there? No. How can he show a round shape up at the top of that cone? Oh, yes. Maybe he makes the shape with his hands! **(Facilitate this)** Now look, we have the cone and the ice cream!*

PRACTICE

1. Partner students. Have them sit "knee-to-knee" and "eye-to-eye" with space between each set of partners. Point out that this is what a Planning Meeting looks like—sitting, facing each other.

2. Guide students through the four steps of creating an ice cream cone—think, share, plan, and create. Emphasize that their ice cream cones do not need to look like the ice cream cone the first group created.

3. Challenge the partners to use the four steps to create other items that could have two parts, for example, a flower, child walking a dog, bird in tree.

Over the next couple of weeks, continue to have students work as partners to create tableaus of other things. The goal is for students to be able to easily work through the four steps without arguing. Each time there is a new challenge, students should be able to quickly and calmly sit in the Planning Meeting position (*i.e., sitting, facing each other*) and complete the four steps. Also, remember to reflect with students about their experience (*see One-Minute Challenge Tableau chapter for reflection ideas*).

EXTEND

1. **Working in Groups of three or four** – Ask students to form Planning Meetings of three or four people. Ask students to recall their first challenge—the ice cream cone. Facilitate students work through the four steps, but now ask them to think about how they could create one ice cream cone with more than two people. How can a group of three or four students still form one picture? If someone says, "I'll be the cone," ask students what would the other two or three students could be? Spend the next few days guiding student groups through several of the same challenges they created earlier (e.g., flower, bird in tree, walking a dog, etc.). Instead of working in partners, they will begin to learn to work in groups of three or four. Students should now understand that three or four people can work together to form one thing.

2. **Add Levels** – Have groups begin to utilize more than one physical level (low, medium, high) in their tableaus.

3. **Broadening the Challenge** – When students can successfully create the given object in partners and groups of three or four, broaden the category of the challenge. Previously, the challenges have involved specific objects (e.g., ice cream cone, flower, etc.). Now begin to give categories (e.g., something people may eat for breakfast, an animal we might see in the zoo, etc.).

    I recommend that you place students in the Observation Deck and invite two strong-thinking students to the Playing Field to model the four steps with the following challenge: Creating a tableau showing something people eat for breakfast.

    • **Think** – *Think about different foods people eat for breakfast. Think of at least three different ideas of foods people may eat for breakfast. Cross your arms once you have an idea.*

- **Share** – Give each person in a group a chance to share one idea. Then, ask each of them to share a second idea. See if the group can come up with at least four different ideas.

- **Plan** – *You have several different ideas—cereal, eggs, bagel, pancakes. WHAT will your tableau show? You can only pick ONE of those ideas. What happens if one person doesn't like that idea? How will you solve this?* (Invite students to share ideas for solving disagreements)

  What PARTS will you need? If you've decided to be pancakes, what parts will you need?

  What part will YOU be? (Ask each student to identify their part. Discuss the possibility that two people might want to be the same thing. Ask students how they would solve the problem.)

- **Create** – Ask each student to describe his or her part. For example, *If you are a pancake, what body shape would you make? Would you be tall or short? If you are the syrup, what body shape would you make? Would you be above or below the pancakes?* (Students create the tableau)

  (Next, invite the class to form Planning Meetings composed of two students. Give them the same challenge, i.e., a type of food people eat for breakfast. Walk through the four steps encouraging them to think of different ideas. Next, give students a different challenge such as something you can find in a classroom.)

  (Continue giving challenges over the next week that involve broader categories. Once students can successfully complete the challenge without arguing, transition them to working in groups of three or four.)

BODY

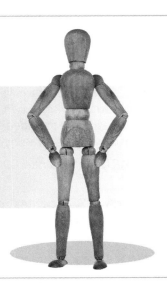

VOICE

IMAGINATION

CONCENTRATION

COOPERATION

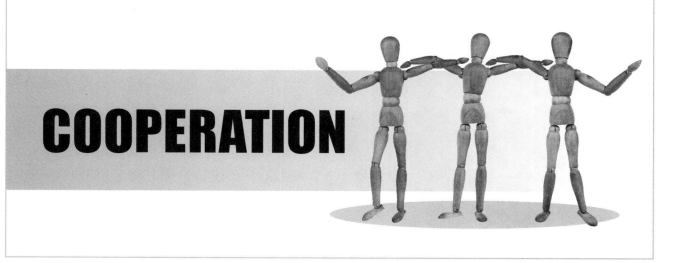

EDUCATOR'S EXPERIENCES: REFLECTIONS FROM THE CLASSROOM

"A mind that is stretched by a new experience can never go back to its old dimensions."

— Oliver Wendell Holmes, Jr.

REFLECTIONS FROM THE CLASSROOM

In this chapter, you will read a range of educators' perspectives about their experiences with Acting Right. These voices include a national consultant for the Acting Right strategies, a principal from an urban school in Washington, D.C., a principal from a school in California with a high ELL population, a beginning teacher, a veteran teacher, and an arts integration curriculum coordinator. They are all from different parts of the country and work with a wide range student populations in a wide range of school environments. They all have a strong commitment to the Acting Right approach to teaching, as they have seen how arts-integrated instruction has transformed their classrooms and schools.

> **Melanie Rick**, national Acting Right consultant
> ***"With this work students are empowered when they know that they have choice."***
>
> *National Board-Certified Teacher, Reading Specialist (MA in Literacy Curriculum and Instruction, BA in Elementary and Special Education), Director and Senior Arts Integration Consultant for Focus 5, Inc.*

Rick has a unique perspective on the Acting Right strategies. She has been a classroom teacher in 3rd, 4th, 6th, and 7th grades as well as an arts integration specialist in a Title I arts magnet school. It was her participation in an Acting Right teacher's workshop over a decade ago that helped her see how behavior was a literacy that she could teach. She now shares the Acting Right strategies with teachers across the nation through Focus 5, Inc.

> **...empowering students to be in control of themselves allowed me to be a more highly effective teacher.**

"I had assumed that students were coming to school knowing how to concentrate and cooperate. I did not realize that the skills of concentration and cooperation were the foundation for building a classroom community where students could work independently and interact effectively in small groups."

"Acting Right strategies changed my entire classroom environment, both for the students and for me. It helped me see that empowering students to be in control of themselves allowed me to be a more highly effective teacher. Teaching became more joyful because I could focus helping the children learn as opposed to just telling them what to do or what I wanted them to know."

As a teacher and teaching coach, Rick has seen Acting Right work at all grade levels, with all types of students, from various demographics, and in various situations. She attributes its overall success to teaching behavior rather than managing it. She believes that concept opens teachers' eyes.

"Accepting the idea that 'Oh, I can teach behavior the same way that I teach other subject areas' can be an Aha! moment," she says. "It can be an epiphany when you realize 'Of course I need to teach behavior. I just hadn't thought of it.'"

"I think that most teachers, who attend the Acting Right professional learning workshops and see it impact students' behavior, are absolutely blown away by the work and see a lot of opportunity and application for their own classrooms. For traditional teachers, it's a bit more challenging for them to adapt to this work. They're hesitant to get the students out of their seats, moving and working together, and concerned about the talking that generates a certain noise level. But they are willing to change their approach to teaching when they see how well the strategies work. Also, it's helpful when teachers are reflective about their practices and really want to build their students' behavioral literacy. These teachers are willing to put themselves in that vulnerable place, to take the risk and begin to change. If they see themselves as a facilitator of learning then they do really well."

Sonia Aramburo, principal and **Sam Tidwell**, first grade teacher
"Our students are no longer passive."

Mary Chapa Academy, Greenfield, CA; 885 students in TK through 5th grade; Turnaround Arts school; 95% free and reduced-price lunch; 78% English-language learners; nearly 25% indigenous families, many of low socioeconomic status.

Mary Chapa Academy was once focused strictly on a traditional academic curriculum. Pencils and paper. No crayons. No arts. When the school became one of the President's Committee on the Arts and Humanities Turnaround Arts schools, principal Sonia Aramburo and two of her colleagues attended an Acting Right workshop at a summer retreat. They liked the fundamental premise of students learning to control themselves and working together as a team through the arts. Over the course of three years, the school participated in on-going professional development focused on the Acting Right strategies.

Mary Chapa Academy is now a very different school.

"Acting Right has allowed us to bring the arts into instruction to help the students access core content," Aramburo says. "It was a fantastic gift to our school. Many of our students are from low socioeconomic situations, and their parents work long hours picking crops in the field. Many of our students don't get learn about behavior at home. My goal is to get every teacher in our school using the strategies. Even our after-school program coordinator is using these practices. That way when the children leave school, they don't lose that structure. We have a lot of English-language learners, and you find them taking ownership of their teams, not just thinking of themselves. It's a challenge for them and they love it."

When she leads assemblies, Aramburo uses the Acting Right vocabulary. She says, "Show you're in control of your bodies." "Make me your focal point." When she visits a classroom to present student-of-the-month honors, she directs the class to make that student their focal point. She says students now stay focused; they know they are in control, and they are not going to let an outside force make them lose focus.

One of the things principal Aramburo values about Acting Right is the development of thinking skills.

"Students are being challenged in their thinking. Traditionally, you provide instruction, check for understanding, and then you find that the students haven't learned it. That's because they're not with you. They're just passive learners. Now, our students are no longer passive. They're active learners and they really enjoy it. There's a lot of research coming out about mindful strategies and how useful they are in learning. The benefits of these strategies have progressed where I can walk into a room and the students stay focused. It's a powerful tool for them."

Sam Tidwell, a first-grade teacher, is relatively new to teaching. What's more, he came to Mary Chapa Academy at mid-year with no teaching experience. The school was struggling with a "revolving door" of teachers leaving the school; the first grade alone had lost three teachers. Desperate for a good teacher, Aramburo asked Tidwell, her neighbor, if he would consider teaching. He accepted. Tidwell reflects on those early days:

"I had no idea how to teach. I'd never taught before. I was scared going into the classroom. I was horrified by my inability to read my students and have any authority whatsoever. It was a madhouse every time I went into that classroom."

Tidwell recalled observing Sean Layne leading the Acting Right strategies with his class.

"What was so beautiful was the way Sean took them and melded them into a single unified team, which because of my inexperience, I had no ability to do. I saw all the social barriers melt away between the boys and girls. He took all of their differences and just swirled them together into a team. The experience was so powerful that I teared up and had to step out of the classroom for a moment. I saw the invisible barriers between my students dissolve in a moment. I knew I needed to learn how to unify my students."

> **"Acting Right is a more benevolent and powerful form of classroom management because it relies on the students to understand why they should choose to behave a certain way in class."**

Tidwell feels fortunate to have encountered the Acting Right approach at the start of his career. Today he is an enthusiastic teacher who has embraced the Acting Right strategies. He uses the Actor's Toolbox four or five times a day—when his students arrive in the morning, when they return from recess and lunch, and anytime he wants to assess their readiness to learn. He recognizes the fallacy of the conventional notion that problem behavior should be suppressed.

"Acting Right is a more benevolent and powerful form of classroom management because it relies on the students to understand why they should choose to behave a certain way in class," Tidwell says. *"It treats them like human beings. It respects their ability to choose. I like that because they need to know, even at a young age, that the decisions they make are important. They need to understand that the choices we make affect our lives, and not just our lives, but the lives of our team. They have to learn to work together."*

Carrie Chinners, fourth grade teacher

"Acting Right completely changed the way I teach."

H.E. Bonner Elementary School, Moncks Corner, SC, a rural area near Charleston, SC; 800 students in K3 through 5th grade; 82% receive free and reduced-price lunch; student population is racially mixed, lower- and middle-class families; students come from five neighboring communities.

Fourth-grade teacher Carrie Chinners, who is now also a part-time trainer for the Acting Right strategies, was accustomed to setting the agenda in her classroom. She would make all the decisions—what the class would learn in the morning and what they would learn in the afternoon. Now, on occasion at least, her 9-year-old students are setting the agenda. And that's just fine with her.

"We do the Concentration Challenge at the beginning of the year to strengthen those muscles. Now that they've developed those concentration muscles, we play it as a reminder, more than a necessity. My students are so in tune with their own behavior that they might say, 'Ms. Chinners, can we play a few levels of the Concentration Challenge, because we need it.' So, we'll do it. They know how to concentrate, but, for example, we'll play the game because it's the week after spring break and they're a little antsy, or it's just one of those days and we're having a hard time staying focused."

Such behavior provides a solid foundation for learning, which Chinners says is a welcome departure from the "sit and get" conventional approach to teaching, where the teacher is at the front of the room delivering information.

"Acting Right challenges the paradigm that learning is solitary and makes you realize how powerful learning is when it's social. This work forces students to be social, which I love because true learning happens when we communicate, not just with our teacher, but with our peers. Sometimes, students are better teachers than their teachers. Students who really understand something can explain it to other students in their own language."

Chinners starts the day with the Actor's Toolbox. She uses the Cooperation Challenge every time she makes groups. She remembers the days when grouping students ignited outbursts of student complaints about their classmates. Now she has none of that, because she has built a cooperative classroom. She uses the One-Minute Challenge Tableau daily – in reading, in science, in social studies.

"I use the One-Minute Challenge Tableaus as starters for the lesson if we need to review what we learned yesterday. I also use them at the close of lessons to wrap up what we've learned. They're quick assessments for me to see if my students are getting what I need them to understand."

Chinners, who has a master's degree in arts integration, has always led an arts-integrated classroom. But she believes that Acting Right has transformed her approach to teaching. She has become more of a facilitator of learning.

"I'm not at all a traditional teacher. If you were to walk by my room, you'd think, 'What are they doing in there?' But you'd realize my students are all on task. They all are smiling and having a good time, but they're all working and learning. I think the thing

that I've learned the most from the Acting Right work is that my students are my team and we're all in this together. When one of us fails, we all fail. When one of us succeeds, we all succeed."

Winston Cox, principal
"It's very pragmatic, but it looks magical."

Noyes Elementary School, Washington, DC; 200 students in pre-K through 5th grade; Turnaround Arts school; Title 1 school, nearly 100% receive free and reduced-price lunch; nearly 100% African-American with increasing number of Central and South American students, many of whom live in three neighboring public housing developments.

Noyes Elementary School has a morning routine as students arrive for the day. Principal Winston Cox says the routine gives students an essential opportunity to calm and settle themselves for the school day. The routine begins with breakfast. Next, the school's physical education teacher leads activities, including the Actor's Toolbox, before students leave for their classrooms.

"I've seen children who came in just look glum and sad. They may have been hungry from the weekend or they may have slept in two or three places over the course of the weekend. And then within 15 minutes, they've had a hot breakfast, they've joined their peers, they've done the Actor's Toolbox, and I've seen what a difference it makes in the beginning of their school day. I've been in this work long enough to know what works and what is just novelty. Acting Right strategies work and they are very powerful."

Cox first encountered Acting Right following a critical moment in the school's development. It was downsizing from a K-8 school to a K-5 school, and with that, the opportunity to rebrand themselves. Cox and his team decided that the arts were going to be the essential component of their identity.

"We had a lot of disconnection and students not feeling excited about school. Many of our families experience intensive, socio-emotional issues, like trauma, generational poverty, and substance abuse. I have an arts background and I knew that the arts had the power to heighten the level of student engagement."

Cox participated in a professional learning retreat and was inspired by an Acting Right workshop. It addressed the need for the active brain, which was critical to Cox, as he had seen how trauma could cause students to be closed and unreceptive to learning. Acting Right could create the calm, centeredness, and balance that he knew his students needed in order to learn.

"It was very clear that philosophically and pragmatically, Acting Right fit in with our identity. All the strategies are really strong pedagogically. Right away I just knew that the strategies were going to be of value to us as a school."

Cox has seen the Concentration Circle help students, with diagnosed and undiagnosed attention deficit challenges as well as those students having a hard time focusing, to develop the capacity to slow down and find a focal point. He has observed how the Cooperation

Challenge can turn the conflict, and aggression that once accompanied the grouping of students, into an environment where all students can work together.

Acting Right is the research-based curriculum Cox embraced as a foundation for his school. He says:

"The strategies are all predicated on the firm conviction that every child is capable of growing. The strategies are routines and practices that anybody can learn. It's very pragmatic, but it looks magical. Brain research is an area of interest to me. I have learned how trauma can cause a brain orientation that is not receptive to learning. The Acting Right approach shows us how to create the calm, centeredness, and balance that students need in order to be able to access the curriculum."

Cox doesn't just take his own perspective into account. Perhaps most importantly, he listens to the students.

"There's an annual student survey given by our school district. There was a profound difference between the year before Acting Right was implemented and the year after. We had unbelievable growth. The survey gives us many strong indicators. Students across the board said they felt that their teachers were making learning more fun and more engaging and that they felt a real connection to the curriculum in a way that they hadn't before."

Rae Takemoto, arts integration curriculum coordinator
"On a scale of 1 to 10, I'd say it's an 11."

Pomaika'i Elementary School in Maui, HI; 585 students in Pre-K through 5th grade; Turnaround Arts school; middle-class neighborhood public school; student population is racially mixed with higher Asian representation.

Rae Takemoto sees Acting Right as more than a teaching strategy or an assessment tool, and it's certainly more than a set of games. She says:

"If you do Acting Right strategies with children at a young age, the wiring in their brain gets stronger and stronger, and they're able to sustain focus. You see that translate to everything. That's a life skill."

Indeed, self-awareness, self-regulation, and the concentration, cooperation, and collaboration "muscles" that Acting Right develops are invaluable tools for the rest of students' academic careers, for their entry into the workforce, and for their interpersonal relationships.

Pomaika'i Elementary School's curriculum is rooted in arts integration. Encountering Acting Right at a professional learning institute led Takemoto to recognize the potential of the strategies to get the entire faculty aligned with the school's mission of arts integration. Takemoto, an arts integration coach and the Turnaround Arts Hawaii program director, says the strategies were so well designed that she was confident that even a teacher new to arts integration would be able to learn and implement them.

Acting Right has been a school-wide strategy at Pomaika'i since 2007. Takemoto considers the Acting Right strategies to be the school's unifying practice. Every teacher in the school uses the strategies. The shared practice allows teachers to support one another and dive deeper into arts-based learning.

"I believe that when the entire faculty experiences arts integration approaches, like Acting Right, they experience what it feels to be a community. It did that for our school. When we have a shared practice, we can dialog together as a whole school and support each other."

Takemoto says the Acting Right foundation is built in kindergarten and first grade, when teachers introduce students to the strategies. Once the groundwork is laid, students enter second grade knowing how to navigate the Actor's Toolbox, the Concentration Circle, the Cooperation Challenge, and One-Minute Challenge Tableau.

"They can just jump right in on the first day of school. Teachers may re-teach the strategies to set their own classroom expectations, but most students enter second grade having had those experiences."

She feels Acting Right strategies have built an inclusive, collaborative community in every classroom and across the whole school.

"As a result of this work, our students are verbal and articulate, and they're willing to take risks and try out new ideas because the Acting Right structure gives them that safety net. What appeals to me is that it's applicable in any content area and across all grade levels. What also appeals to me is that the strategies involves every child actively. No child is sitting on the sidelines."

Takemoto believes students' grasp of the Acting Right strategies allows them to transition quickly to a calm, focused, and balanced state. They can transition from the playground's high energy to the classroom within seconds and be ready to be a team member and learner.

"Teaching the children to have focus and self-awareness is a powerful thing for them and highly efficient for our teachers. There's so much to do, so we want to put our energy into learning as opposed to trying to manage behaviors."

Rae sums up her assessment of Acting Right simply:

"On a scale of 1 to 10, I'd say it's an 11."

CHAPTER 8

CONCLUSION

"Experience is not what happens to you. It is what you do with what happens to you."

— Aldous Huxley

THE ARTS, THE BRAIN, AND HOW WE LEARN

One of the central themes of this book is that behavior is a literacy, a skill that can be taught, and that like muscles, these skills can be strengthened with repeated use. The Acting Right strategies provide this opportunity.

Scholarly research shows that the arts promote the development of the brain and augment the learning process through repeated application. Eric Jensen, a former educator who is a leader in linking neuroscience to everyday educational practices, writes in his book *Arts with the Brain in Mind* that the arts nurture multiple neurobiological brain systems—the cognitive, emotional, and attentional capacities that are critical foundations of learning [13].

These brain-based capacities are also catalysts for the development of behavioral skills.

I have seen the Acting Right strategies put into practice for decades and I know they work. But through my exploration into cognitive neuroscience, I can tell you why they work. My reading has validated what I knew inherently and repeatedly observed—that the arts wield a powerful influence on the development of the brain and subsequently enhance the capacity not just for learning, but for making strong choices about one's own behavior that in turn promote learning.

> " — the arts wield a powerful influence on the development of the brain and subsequently enhance the capacity not just for learning, but for making strong choices about one's own behavior which in turn promote learning. "

Perhaps I can best illustrate how an environment supports the development of multiple brain systems by showing you what does not work. For example, young children have fundamental needs—emotional and social stability, healthy interpersonal attachments, the opportunity to learn and explore in a supportive environment—all of which impact optimal brain development. Meeting these basic needs is severely compromised in impoverished families, where teenage motherhood, poor healthcare, unstable environments, and other factors are present.

Eric Jensen, also the author of *Teaching with Poverty in Mind*, maintains that unmet needs, such as "a strong, reliable primary caregiver who provides consistent and unconditional love, guidance, and support" and "enrichment through personalized, increasingly complex activities," have neurological consequences. He writes, "Deficits in these areas inhibit the production of new brain cells, alter the path of maturation, and rework the healthy neural circuitry in children's brains, thereby undermining emotional and social development and predisposing them to emotional dysfunction [14]."

As a result, many children raised in poverty come to the classroom with issues, such as poor emotional regulation, inappropriate emotional responses, the inability to work cooperatively in groups, and deficiencies in politeness, respect, and the so-called social graces. Interestingly, Jensen concludes that we must teach the positive behaviors to at-risk students. It affirms again that behavior does not need to be managed; it needs to be taught.

What works in supporting the developing brain is, among other pedagogical methods, an arts-integrated learning environment that empowers students to navigate complex issues, make strong choices, and think for themselves. Strategies, like those practiced by Acting Right, establish the basis for an art-integrated learning environment.

Many approaches to arts-integrated instruction integrate activities that research in neuro-science shows aids retention of information. Mariale Hardiman, a former educator and the author of *The Brain-Targeted Teaching Model for 21st Century Schools*, writes that arts-based activities allow students to reinforce their understanding through emotional expression.

"Any form of artistic activity has the potential to forge emotional connections to content that are richer and more rewarding than those achieved using conventional teaching strategies," Hardiman says. "The arts encourage provocative questions, careful observations, exploration of multiple viewpoints, and new modes of interpretation [15]."

As Hardiman says, and as Acting Right has demonstrated, incorporating arts-based activities into instruction typically enhances comprehension and long-term memory of material. It also encourages sustained attention to tasks like the focus students learn and achieve when participating in the Actor's Toolbox and the Concentration Challenge.

Hardiman eschews an excessive reliance on traditional instruction that creates passive learners, as is the case with instruction that is delivered solely in written or oral form. She maintains that students' retention of information is significantly improved when they generate that information in response to a prompt. The One-Minute Challenge Tableau provides a concrete example for achieving that retention.

THE CLASSROOM TRANSFORMED

Clearly the impact of the Acting Right strategies stretches beyond the realm of drama. They develop students' thinking, social, and learning skills, specifically imagination, coopera-tion, concentration and the control of body and voice. These skills and abilities aid in learning across subjects. Further, through Acting Right strategies, students learn to work together as a team, balance their energy for learning, and grow stronger in their ability to focus their attention without giving in to external and internal distractions. The arts are not only an important outlet for student expression, they develop valuable skills that increase the likeli-hood of student success.

As you implement these strategies in your classroom, know that the time you invest will be beneficial for days, weeks, months, even years to come. You will spend less time disciplining and managing behavior and more time teaching. Students will spend less time struggling to attain negative attention through misbehavior and more time engaging and learning. Teaching behavior as a literacy will result in stronger academic achievement, as more students will be able to focus and concentrate on their work.

The power and beauty of Acting Right is in the transformation of classrooms, or more accurately, the transformation in students. As I have worked to develop these strategies and teach them to educators across the country, what has propelled me forward are the positive responses from educators regarding the changes these strategies have created in their students' behavior. I remember the teacher, a 25-year veteran of the classroom, who told me she had never seen anything like this transformation happen in her career and she needed to know how I did it. For years, I have been working to uncover how and why the

CONCLUSION

strategies work. I have come to the conclusion that my work will never be totally finished and as time passes, and new children enter our education system, I will continue to develop and improve the strategies.

My mission is to help educators understand that there are strategies that can help them achieve a calm, balanced, and focused classroom of students ready for learning. My mission is also to continue to develop approaches to teaching through the arts that build students' ability to concentrate on their work, collaborate effectively with those around them, and ultimately, to experience being empowered with the knowledge that behavior is always their choice.

NOTES

[1] Line Goguen-Hughes, "Mindfulness and Learning: What's the Connection?" *Mindful*. 19 April 2011. https://www.mindful.org/mindfulness-and-learning-whats-the-connection/ Accessed 19 February 2017.

[2] Dr. Payel Banarjee, Kamlesh Kumar , "A Study on Self-Regulated Learning and Academic Achievement" *IJMAS, International Journal of Multidisciplinary Approach and Studies, Vol 01, No.6, Nov-Dec 2014* http://ijmas.com/upcomingissue/26.06.14.pdf. Accessed 19 February 2017.

[3] Geoffrey Caine, Renate N Caine, Making Connections: *Teaching and the Human Brain*, (Lebanon, IN: Dale Seymour Publications, part of the Pearson Learning Group, 1994),

[4] Judy Willis, M.D., M. Ed, practiced neurology for 20 years; she currently teaches at Santa Barbara Middle School in California and conducts professional development workshops. She is the author of Teaching the Brain to Read: Strategies for Improving Fluency, Vocabulary, and Comprehension (ASCD, 2008); www.RADTeach.com; jwillisneuro@aol.com

[5] Paula Denton. "The Power of Our Words." *Educational Leadership*, (Alexandra, VA: AASA-American Association of School Administrators, Volume 66, No 1, September 2008). http://www.ascd.org/publications/educational-leadership/sept08/vol66/num01/The-Power-of-Our-Words.aspx. Accessed 8 March 2017

[6] Sondra H. Birch, Gary W. Ladd, The teacher-child relationship and children's early school adjustment, Journal of School Psychology, Volume 35, Issue 1, 1997, Pages 61-79, ISSN 0022-4405, http://dx.doi.org/10.1016/S0022-4405(96)00029-5. (http://www.sciencedirect.com/science/article/pii/S0022440596000295) Keywords: Teacher-child relationships; School adjustment; Children Accessed 8 March 2017

[7] Daniel Goleman, Focus: *The Hidden Driver of Excellence.* (New York: HarperCollins, 2013)

[8] Sharon Zumbrunn, Joseph Tadlock, Elizabeth Danielle Roberts, "Encouraging Self-Regulated Learning in the Classroom: A Review of the Literature," *Metropolitan Educational Research Consortium (MERC), Virginia Commonwealth University,* (October 2011)

[9] Mariale M. Hardiman, *The Brain-Targeted Teaching Model for 21st Century Schools,* (Thousand Oaks, CA: Corwin Press, A SAGE Publishing Company, 2012): pages 50-51.

[10] Robert E. Slavin, "Making Cooperative Learning Powerful," *Educational Leadership*, (Alexandra, VA: ASCD-Association for Supervision and Curriculum Development, 2014) http://www.ascd.org/publications/educational-leadership/oct14/vol72/num02/Making-Cooperative-Learning-Powerful.aspx. Accessed 6 March 2017.

[11] David A.Sousa." How the Arts Develop the Young Brain", *The School Administrator by AASA-American Association of School Administrators,* Volume 63, No 11, December 2006), http://www.aasa.org/Publications-and-Online-Media/. Also published on: http://www.carolinaschoolforinquiry.com/newsArticles/How_The_Arts_Develop_The_Young_Brain_12_06.pdf. Accessed 15 May 2017.

[12] David A. Sousa, How the Brain Learns, (Thousand Oaks, CA: Corwin Press, A SAGE Publishing Company, 2011)

[13] Eric Jensen, *Arts with the Brain in Mind*, (Alexandra, VA: ASCD-Association for Supervision and Curriculum Development, 2001)

[14] Eric Jensen. *Teaching with Poverty in Mind*, (Alexandra, VA: ASCD-Association for Supervision and Curriculum Development, 2009)

[15] Mariale M. Hardiman, *The Brain-Targeted Teaching Model for 21st Century Schools*, (Thousand Oaks, CA: Corwin Press, A SAGE Publishing Company, 2012)

WORKS CITED

Goguen-Hughes, Line. "Mindfulness and Learning: What's the Connection?" *Mindful*. (19 April 2011) https://www.mindful.org/mindfulness-and-learning-whats-the-connection/. Accessed 10 March 2017.

Goleman, Daniel. *Focus: The Hidden Driver of Excellence*. (New York: HarperCollins, 2013) Hardiman, Mariale M., & Scientific Research Publishing Inc. Creative Education, 2016, 7, 1913-1928 Published Online 26 August 2016 in SciRes. http://www.scirp.org/journal/ce http://dx.doi.org/10.4236/ce.2016.714194. Accessed 10 March 2017.

Hardiman, Mariale M. *The Brain-Targeted Teaching Model for 21st Century Schools*, (Thousand Oaks, CA: Corwin Press, A SAGE Publishing Company, 2012)

Jensen, Eric. *Arts with the Brain in Mind*, (Alexandra, VA: ASCD-Association for Supervision and Curriculum Development, 2001)

Jensen, Eric. *Teaching with Poverty in Mind*, (Alexandra, VA: ASCD-Association for Supervision and Curriculum Development, 2009)

Schindler, John. *Transformative Classroom Management: Positive Strategies to Engage All Students and Promote a Psychology of Success*, (San Francisco, CA: Jossey-Bass, A Wiley Imprint, 2010)

Schwartz, Katrina. "Age of Distraction: Why It's Crucial for Students to Learn to Focus," *KQED Mind-Shift*, (December 5, 2013) https://ww2.kqed.org/mindshift/2013/12/05/age-of-distraction-why-its-crucial-for-students-to-learn-to-focus/. Accessed 17 February 2017.

Sinha, Kirin. "Kinesthetic Learning: Moving Toward a New Model for Education," *Edutopia.org, A George Lucas Educational Foundation*. (July 24, 2014) https://www.edutopia.org/blog/kinesthetic-learning-new-model-education-kirin-sinha. Accessed 7 February 2017.

Slavin, Robert E. "Making Cooperative Learning Powerful," Educational Leadership Journal, (Alexandra, VA: ASCD-Association for Supervision and Curriculum Development, 2014) http://www.ascd.org/publications/educational-leadership/oct14/vol72/num02/Making-Cooperative-Learning-Powerful.aspx. Accessed 6 March 2017.

Slavin, Robert E. "Synthesis of Research on Cooperative Learning," *Educational Leadership Journal,* (Alexandra, VA: ASCD-Association for Supervision and Curriculum Development, Febru-ary,1991) http://www.ascd.org/ASCD/pdf/journals/ed_lead/el_199102_slavin.pdf . Accessed 6 March 2017.

Sousa, David. "How the Arts Develop the Young Brain," *The School Administrator by AASA- American Association of School Administrators*, December 2006/, Volume 63/ Number 11), http://www.aasa.org/SchoolAdministratorArticle.aspx?id=7378; Republished in: http://www.carolinaschoolforinquiry.com/newsArticles/How_The_Arts_Develop_The_Young_Brain_12_06.pdf. Accessed 6 March 2017.

Zumbrunn, Sharon, Tadlock, Joseph, Roberts, Elizabeth Danielle. "Encouraging Self-Regulated Learning in the Classroom: A Review of the Literature." *Metropolitan Educational Research Consortium* (MERC), Virginia Commonwealth University, (October 2011)

SUGGESTED READING

Eric Jensen, *Arts with the Brain in Mind*, (Alexandra, VA: ASCD-Association for Supervision and Curriculum Development, 2001)

Cesar Millan, Melissa Jo Peltier, *Be the Pack Leader*, (New York: Three Rivers Press, an imprint of the Crown Publishing Group, a division of Random House, Inc., 2007)

Alfie Kohn, Beyond Discipline: *From Compliance to Community* (Alexandra, VA: ASCD-Association for Supervision and Curriculum Development; First Edition, 1996; 10th Anniversary (Second) Edition, 2006)

William Glasser, M.D., *Choice Theory in the Classroom* (New York: HarperCollins Publishers, Inc. 1986)

Rick Smith, *Conscious Classroom Management: Unlocking the Secrets of Great Teaching*, (Sherman Oaks, CA: Corwin Press, A SAGE Publishing Company, 2004); First Edition

Becky A. Bailey, *Conscious Discipline: 7 Basic Skills for Brain Smart Classroom Management*, (Oviedo, FL: Loving Guidance, Inc, 2001)

Becky A. Bailey, *Conscious Discipline: 7 Basic Skills for Brain Smart Classroom Management, Expanded and Updated: Building Resilient Classrooms*, (Oviedo, FL: Loving Guidance, Inc, 2015)

David W. Johnson, Roger T. Johnson and Edythe Johnson Holubec, *Cooperation in the Classroom* (Alexandra, VA: ASCD-Association for Supervision and Curriculum Development, 1994; 7th Edition, 1998; 8th Edition, 2008)

David A. Sousa, *Educational Neuroscience*, (Thousand Oaks, CA: Corwin Press, A SAGE Publishing Company, 2011)

Viola Spolin, *Theatre Games for the Classroom: A Teacher's Handbook*, (Evanston, IL: Northwestern University Press, 1986) First Edition

Rick Smith, Grace Dearborn, *Conscious Classroom Management: Unlocking the Secrets of Great Teaching II*, (Fairfax, CA: Conscious Teaching Publications, 2016); Second Edition

Daniel Goleman, *Emotional Intelligence: Why It Can Matter More than IQ*, (New York: Bantam Books, 1995)

John L. Luckner and Reldan S. Nadler, *Processing the Experience: Strategies to Enhance and Generalize Learning* (Dubuquee, IA: Kendall/Hunt Publishing Company, 1997)

Jim Fay and David Funk, *Teaching with Love and Logic: Taking Control of the Classroom*, (Golden, CO: Love and Logic Institute, Inc, 2010)

David A. Sousa, *How the Brain Influences Behavior: Strategies for Managing K-12 Classrooms*, (Thousand Oaks, CA: Corwin Press, A SAGE Publishing Company, 2015)

David A. Sousa, *How the Brain Influences Behavior: Management Strategies for Every Classroom*, (Thousand Oaks, CA: Corwin Press, A SAGE Publishing Company, 2009)

Viola Spolin, Mary Ann Brandt, Arthur Morey, *Theatre Games for the Classroom: A Teacher's Handbook*, (Evanston, IL: Northwestern University Press, 1997) Second Edition

Fredric Jones, Patrick T. Jones, Brian T. Jones, T*ools for Teaching: Discipline* Instruction*Motivation: Primary Prevention of Discipline Problems*, (Santa Cruz, CA: Fredric H Jones & Associates, Inc, 2007)

Mariale M. Hardiman, *The Brain-Targeted Teaching Model for 21st Century Schools*, (Thousand Oaks, CA: Corwin Press, A SAGE Publishing Company, 2012); Check out the free study guide at http://braintargetedteaching.org/

David Sousa, "How the Arts Develop the Young Brain", *The School Administrator by AASA- American Association of School Administrators*, Volume 63, No 11, December 2006), http://www.aasa.org/Publications-and-Online-Media/ http://www.carolinaschoolforinquiry.com/newsArticles/How_The_Arts_Develop_The_Young_Brain_12_06.pdf

David A. Sousa, *How the Brain Learns*, (Thousand Oaks, CA: Corwin Press, A SAGE Publishing Company, 2011)

Mariale M. Hardiman, Education and the Arts: Educating Every Child in the Spirit of Inquiry and Joy. *Creative Education*, 7, 1913-1928. (2016) http://dx.doi.org/10.4236/ce.2016.714194

https://www.edutopia.org/blog/brain-breaks-focused-attention-practices-lori-desautels

http://www.ala.org/alsc/sites/ala.org.alsc/files/content/compubs/booklists/comfortingreads/170523_ALSC_Booklist_ComfortingReads_FINAL_Pages.pdf

https://www.edutopia.org/blog/strategies-strengthening-brains-executive-functions-donna-wilson-marcus-conyers

http://www.edweek.org/ew/articles/2017/05/17/children-must-be-taught-to-collaborate-studies.html

http://www.p21.org/storage/documents/Skills_For_Today_Series-Pearson/Educators_-_Executive_Summary_FINAL.pdf http://www.p21.org/storage/documents/Skills_For_Today_Series-Pearson/Educators_-_Executive_Summary_FINAL.pdf

http://www.ascd.org/publications/educational-leadership/oct14/vol72/num02/Making-Cooperative-Learning-Powerful.aspx (October 2014/Volume 72/Number2/ Instructions That Sticks): Pages 22-26

Cunningham, Aimee. "Kids' Self-Control Is Crucial for Their Future Success", *Scientific American Mind, part of Spring Nature, 1945-Present.* (1 July 2011). https://www.scientificamerican.com/article/where-theres-a-will/

Sparks, Sarah D. "Children Must Be Taught to Collaborate, Studies Say: Researchers explore group work in class." *Education Week*. Bethseda, Maryland: Editorial Projects in Education. (May 26, 2017). http://www.edweek.org/ew/articles/2017/05/17/children-must-be-taught-to-collaborate-studies.html?print=1.

ARTS INTEGRATION

creativity
cooperation
collaboration
instruction
focus
tableau
drama
education

FOCUS 5
music writing & drama & art & dance &

Focus 5, Inc. provides high quality professional learning opportunities and program consulting focused on aligning arts integration, best instructional practices, and current thinking in the field of arts and education.

Visit ArtsIntegrationConsulting.com for more information about:

- Acting Right consultants that can work with the students and staff at your school.
  Check out the About Us tab for more information

- Other arts integration strategies *Focus 5, Inc.* offers.
  Check out the Professional Learning tab for more information

- Ordering Acting Right resources such as:
  - Music CD for Actor's Toolbox
  - Jewels of Concentration for the Concentration Circle
  - One-Minute Challenge Tableau classroom poster
  - Laminated facilitator cards
  - Acting Right Catch Phrase classroom poster set
  - Additional resources like podcasts, videos, instructional examples, and more

Website: ArtsIntegrationConsulting.com
Follow Acting Right on Facebook: Type Acting Right in the search bar
Twitter: @sblayne